Frommer's®

Seoul
day BY day®

1st Edition

by Cecilia Hae-Jin Lee

WILEY

Wiley Publishing, Inc.

Contents

Published by:

Wiley Publishing, Inc.

111 River St.
Hoboken, NJ 07030-5774

ISBN: 978-0-470-93144-8 (paper); 978-1-118-08935-4 (ebk); 978-1-118-08934-7 (ebk); 978-1-118-08933-0 (ebk)

Editor: Jamie Ehrlich
Production Editor: Michael Brumitt
Photo Editor: Richard Fox
Cartographer: Tim Lohnes
Production by Wiley Indianapolis Composition Services

Front cover photos, left to right: N Tower © Will & Deni McIntyre / PhotoLibrary; rice cakes © Anthony Plummer / Lonely Planet Images; Neon lights © Urbanmyth / Alamy Images

Back cover photo: Space Café Oi interior © Cho Seong Joon / Aurora Photos

For information on our other products and services or to obtain technical support, please contact our Customer Care Department within the U.S. at 877/762-2974, outside the U.S. at 317/572-3993 or fax 317/572-4002.

Wiley also publishes its books in a variety of electronic formats. Some content that appears in print may not be available in electronic formats.

Manufactured in China

5   4   3   2   1

A Note from the Editorial Director

Organizing your time. That's what this guide is all about.

Other guides give you long lists of things to see and do and then expect you to fit the pieces together. The Day by Day guides are different. These guides tell you the best of everything, and then they show you how to see it *in the smartest, most time-efficient way*. Our authors have designed detailed itineraries organized by time, neighborhood, or special interest. And each tour comes with a bulleted map that takes you from stop to stop.

Hoping to wander Seoul's streets or haggle at its many popular markets? Planning to learn more about Korea's rich history, or eat your way through the city? Whatever your interest or schedule, the Day by Days give you the smartest routes to follow. Not only do we take you to the top attractions, hotels, and restaurants, but we also help you access those special moments that locals get to experience—those "finds" that turn tourists into travelers.

The Day by Days are also your top choice if you're looking for one complete guide for all your travel needs. The best hotels and restaurants for every budget, the greatest shopping values, the wildest nightlife—it's all here.

Why should you trust our judgment? Because our authors personally visit each place they write about. They're an independent lot who say what they think and would never include places they wouldn't recommend to their best friends. They're also open to suggestions from readers. If you'd like to contact them, please send your comments our way at feedback@frommers.com, and we'll pass them on.

Enjoy your Day by Day guide—the most helpful travel companion you can buy. And have the trip of a lifetime.

Warm regards,

Kelly Regan

Kelly Regan, Editorial Director
Frommer's Travel Guides

About the Author

Cecilia Hae-Jin Lee was born in Seoul and is the author of several popular books on Korea, including *Quick & Easy Korean Cooking* and *Eating Korean: From Barbeque to Kimchi Recipes from My Home*. She is the author of *Frommer's South Korea*. She is also a conceptual and installation artist, a designer, an illustrator, and a photographer. Her first and third language is Korean.

Acknowledgments

Special thanks to my Jumi-imo for her research and constant assistance and for the rest of my extended family in Seoul, who is always generous in opening their home. Thanks also to Jamie Ehrlich for getting this manuscript into shape and my husband Tim for taking care of everything, while Seoul consumed me for months at a time.

An Additional Note

Please be advised that travel information is subject to change at any time—and this is especially true of prices. We therefore suggest that you write or call ahead for confirmation when making your travel plans. The authors, editors, and publisher cannot be held responsible for the experiences of readers while traveling. Your safety is important to us, however, so we encourage you to stay alert and be aware of your surroundings.

Star Ratings, Icons & Abbreviations

Every hotel, restaurant, and attraction listing in this guide has been ranked for quality, value, service, amenities, and special features using a **star-rating system.** Hotels, restaurants, attractions, shopping, and nightlife are rated on a scale of zero stars (recommended) to three stars (exceptional). In addition to the star-rating system, we also use a **kids** icon to point out the best bets for families. Within each tour, we recommend cafes, bars, or restaurants where you can take a break. Each of these stops appears in a shaded box marked with a coffee-cup-shaped bullet ☕.

The following **abbreviations** are used for credit cards:

AE	American Express	DISC	Discover	V	Visa
DC	Diners Club	MC	MasterCard		

Travel Resources at Frommers.com

Frommer's travel resources don't end with this guide. Frommer's web-site, **www.frommers.com**, has travel information on more than 4,000 destinations. We update features regularly, giving you access to the most current trip-planning information and the best airfare, lodging, and car-rental bargains. You can also listen to podcasts, connect with other Frommers.com members through our active-reader forums, share your travel photos, read blogs from guidebook editors and fellow travelers, and much more.

A Note on Prices

In the "Take a Break" and "Best Bets" sections of this book, we have used a system of dollar signs to show a range of costs for 1 night in a hotel (the price of a double-occupancy room) or the cost of an entree at a restaurant. Use the following table to decipher the dollar signs:

Cost	Hotels	Restaurants
$	under $100	under $10
$$	$100–$200	$10–$20
$$$	$200–$300	$20–$30
$$$$	$300–$400	$30–$40
$$$$$	over $400	over $40

How to Contact Us

In researching this book, we discovered many wonderful places—hotels, restaurants, shops, and more. We're sure you'll find others. Please tell us about them, so we can share the information with your fellow travelers in upcoming editions. If you were disappointed with a recommendation, we'd love to know that, too. Please write to:

Frommer's Seoul Day by Day, 1st Edition
Wiley Publishing, Inc. • 111 River St. • Hoboken, NJ 07030-5774
frommersfeedback@wiley.com

10 Favorite
Moments

10 Favorite **Moments**

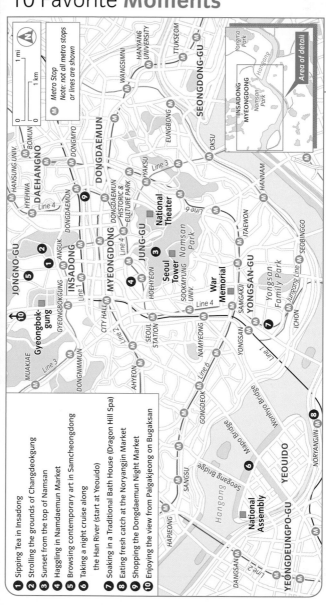

Metro Stop: not all metro stops or lines are shown

1 Sipping Tea in Insadong
2 Strolling the grounds of Changdeokgung
3 Sunset from the top of Namsan
4 Haggling in Namdaemun Market
5 Browsing contemporary art in Samcheongdong
6 Taking a night cruise along the Han River (start at Yeouido)
7 Soaking in a Traditional Bath House (Dragon Hill Spa)
8 Eating fresh catch at the Noryangjin Market
9 Shopping the Dongdaemun Night Market
10 Enjoying the view from Palgakjeong on Bugaksan

Previous page: A view of the city from Bongeunsa temple.

Don't judge a city by its cover, or in Seoul's case, usually a thin layer of smog. A closer examination reveals modern sky-scrapers built around ancient palace grounds, crowded traditional markets that operate 24/7, and well-heeled businessmen drinking *soju, Korea's traditional distilled alcohol,* under tarp-covered stalls. Hidden among the honking horns and crowded subways are some of our favorite places to visit and experience in this ever-changing city.

A traditional tea shop in Insadong.

1 **Sipping tea in Insadong.** You can almost taste a bit of the Joseon Dynasty in the old arts district. Most of the traditional teashops here are converted *hanok* (traditional houses) or made to look like one. Choose one tucked into winding alleys or view the pedestrian traffic below from a second-floor vantage point. *See p 35.*

2 **Strolling the grounds of Changdeokgung and Biwon.** Though not the largest of the five palaces in the city, Changdeokgung is the best designed, built with loca-tion and natural balance in mind. Guided tours of the grounds save the secret garden (Biwon), with its lotus pond and royal plantings, for last. *See p 11.*

3 **Catching the sunset from atop Namsan.** The glowing white N Seoul Tower, perched on top of Namsan, affords the best views of the city. Lovers bring little engraved locks, emblems of their relationships, and leave thousands of them along the edges of the viewing platform. *See p 16.*

The N Seoul Tower atop Namsan.

Food vendors in Gwangjang Market.

4 Haggling in a traditional market. The largest traditional market in the city is Namdaemun Shijang, but Gwangjang Shijang is the oldest. Both are rambling collections of individual vendors hawking everything from housewares and blankets to eyeglasses and clothing. Don't be shy about bargaining down the sellers. *See p 70.*

5 Browsing contemporary art in Samcheong-dong. Only in the past decade has this old neighborhood been allowed to be developed. Now it has galleries and tiny boutiques selling the latest creations of Korean jewelry designers, ceramicists, and painters. *See p 39.*

6 Taking a night cruise along the Han River. After the sun sets, Seoul comes alive. The lights of the city's skyscrapers and bridges reflect along the quiet waters of the Han-gang. It's best to catch the boat off the dock on Yeouido. *See p 124.*

7 Soaking in a traditional bathhouse. Although modern Korean homes are equipped with baths and showers, natives still like to scrub themselves clean at communal bathhouses once a week. Twenty-four-hour *jjimjilbang* can be found in every neighborhood, and modern spas and massage facilities, like the Dragon Hill Spa, are available in Yongsan, Gangnam, and other wealthier parts of town. *See p 27.*

8 Eating fresh catch at the Noryangjin Market. If it's edible and from the ocean, you'll find it at this 24-hour marine products market. Sea creatures burble, wiggle, and slither underwater, waiting to make their way to restaurants and refrigerators all over the city. Come early to see the auction on the second floor and then have a breakfast of *hwae* (raw fish) that you choose from one of the many bubbling tanks. *See p 31.*

9 Shopping the Dongdaemun night market. In a city that never sleeps, bargains can be found at night market where you can shop into the wee hours. Of the many large complexes and open stalls crowded in the area, the multistoried Doota department store is the most popular. *See p 69.*

10 Enjoying the view from Palgakjeong on Bugaksan. Serious hikers will make their way up Bugaksan's steep slopes to see the old fortress walls and the city from Palgakjeong. Those with less time and less hardy dispositions can grab a taxi to the top to enjoy expansive views of Seoul. ●

The Best **in One Day**

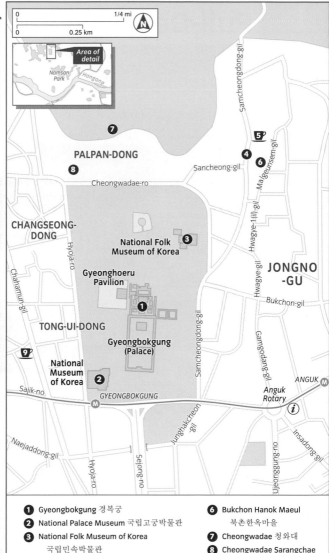

1 Gyeongbokgung 경복궁
2 National Palace Museum 국립고궁박물관
3 National Folk Museum of Korea
  국립민속박물관
4 Samcheongdong-gil 삼청동길
5 Cook'n Heim 쿡앤하임
6 Bukchon Hanok Maeul
  북촌한옥마을
7 Cheongwadae 청와대
8 Cheongwadae Sarangchae
  청와대사랑채
9 Tosokchon 토속촌

Previous page: Jogyesa Temple.

Seoul is a rambling city and impossible to see in one day. But if that's all you have, we suggest you start in the cultural and physical heart of the city. You'll get a sense of Seoul's history and a good blend of the traditional and the new. **Tips:** Wear comfortable shoes, and start your tour at 9am if you want to see the traditional gate opening ceremony. START: **Gyeongbokgung.**

Gyeongbokgung.

❶ ★★ Gyeongbokgung (Gyeongbok Palace). Start at the entrance gate at 9:30am for a free tour in English. Of the palaces built during the Joseon Dynasty, this was the largest and most important. Said to have had 500 buildings, it served as the home of Joseon kings for 200-plus years. During the Japanese colonial period, all but 10 structures were demolished, but many were rebuilt. ⏱ *1 hr. 1 Sejong-no, Jongno-gu.* ☎ *02/3700-3900. www.royalpalace.go.kr/html/eng/data/data_01.jsp?dep1=2. Admission* ₩3,000 ages 19 and over, ₩1,500 ages 7–18. Mar–Oct 9am–6pm; Nov–Feb 9am–5pm; May–Aug Sat–Sun 9am–7pm. Last entry 1 hr. before closing. Closed Tues. Subway: Gyeongbokgung, line 3 (exit 5).

❷ National Palace Museum. Located on the grounds of Gyeongbokgung, the museum has relics from Gyeongbokgung, Changdeokgung, Changgyeonggung, and Jongmyo. Focusing on the Joseon Dynasty (1392–1910), it's the perfect place to learn about Confucianism

National Palace Museum.

National Folk Museum.

(once Korea's main religion), royal ancestral rites, and palace architecture. ⏲ *30 min. Inside the gates of Gyeongbokgung.* ☎ *02/3701-7500. Palace entry includes museum admission. Closed Mon.*

❸ ★ **National Folk Museum of Korea.** As the name suggests, this museum shows the everyday lives of regular Korean people when the country was largely agricultural. ⏲ *45 min. Inside the gates of Gyeongbokgung.* ☎ *02/3704-3114. Free admission. Same hours as Gyeongbokgung.*

❹ ★★ **Samcheongdong-gil.** Stretching up from Gyeongbokgung to Samcheong Park, the main street of this famous area is lined with galleries, cafes, restaurants, and cute

boutiques, many of them converted from *hanok* (traditional houses). Cross the street from the palace and explore the contemporary art galleries along the way. Then veer right up the hill (at Kujje Gallery), where you can explore streets with little shops and fun restaurant facades. ⏲ *1 hr. Samcheongdong-gil starts after a 10-min. uphill walk along the stone wall of Gyeongbokgung. See p. 38 for detailed map of area.*

❺ ★ **Cook'n Heim.** A gallery and cozy white rooms surround a cute hanok courtyard. Freshly made hamburgers, salads, and other Western fare are served with the usual side of potato salad, of course. *63-28 Samcheong-dong.* ☎ *02/733-1109. Daily noon–1pm. $$.*

❻ ★★ **Bukchon Hanok Maeul.** Although most of Seoul's traditional houses have been razed for multistoried apartment complexes, vestiges of a quieter time exist in Bukchon. This hilly neighborhood, full of wood and brick traditional houses with black-tiled roofs, overlooks downtown Seoul and Gyeongbokgung. ⏲ *1 hr. From Samcheongdong-gil, go west on the street with Romanée Conti and then up the road past the*

Cheongwadae.

Bukchon Hanok Maeul.

Pottery Museum. Subway: Anguk, line 3 (exit 2); then bus no. 11 to Donmi pharmacy.

❼ Cheongwadae. South Korea's "Blue House" is home to the president. With advanced reservations you can take a tour (at 3 and 4pm), but anyone can visit the grounds. Be sure to bring your passport. ⏱ *1 hr. 1 Cheongwadae-ro, Jongno-gu. ☎ 02/730-5800. http://english. president.go.kr. Walk through Sam-cheong-dong down to Cheongwadae.*

❽ ★ Cheongwadae Sarangchae. A *sarangchae* in a traditional aristocrat's home was the room where the men of the house entertained visiting men. Of course, this new museum isn't open only to males. It highlights

Korean history (mainly via presidential policy), culture, and UNESCO sites. ⏱ *1–1½ hr. 152 Hyoja-dong, Jongno-gu. ☎ 02/723-0300. www. cwdsarangchae.kr. Free admission. Tues–Sun 9am–6pm; English tours 10am, noon, 2pm, and 4pm. In front of the Cheongwadae fountain.*

❾ ★★ Tosokchon. You can't miss this old-fashioned building near Gyeongbokgung. Famous for their *samgyetang* (stuffed whole chicken soup), they also serve an outstanding *jeongigui tongdak* (whole roasted chicken) and tasty *pajeon* (green-onion flatcakes). *85-1 Chebu-dong, Jongno-gu. ☎ 02/737-7444. M, V. Daily 10am–10pm. $$.*

Visiting Bukchon Hanok Maeul

Not really set up for tourists, the Bukchon Hanok Maeul is a neighborhood set on an incline. Visitors should be respectful of residents while exploring the traditional houses. Those wanting to experience a traditional homestay can make reservations at **Bukchon Guest House** (p 130), **Tea Guest House** (p. 136), or **Seoul Guest House** (p 134). These are traditional homes, modernized with flushing toilets, air-conditioning, and even Internet access. However, they have limited space, so advance planning is highly recommended.

The Best in **Two Days**

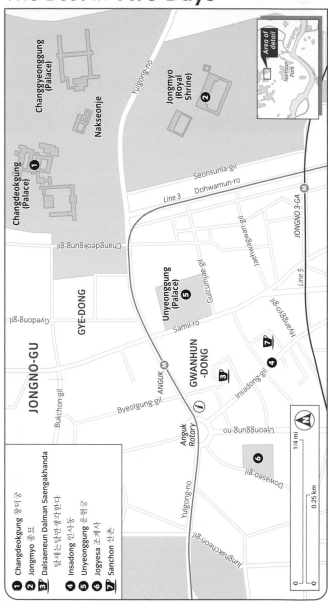

Changgyeonggung (Palace)

Changdeokgung (Palace)

Nakseonje

Jongmyo (Royal Shrine)

2

1

Yulgong-ro

Seonsunla-gil

Line 3

Dohwamun-ro

JONGNO 3-GA

Changdeokgung-gil

Jaehwamun-gil

Line 5

Gyedong-gil

Bukchon-gil

GYE-DONG

JONGNO-GU

Unyeonggung (Palace)

5

Gulcumjae-gil

Samil-ro

Hyangyo-gil

7

3

4

ANGUK

GWANHUN -DONG

Insadong-gil

Byeolgung-gil

Anguk Rotary

(i)

Uleonggung-no

6

Dowaseo-gil

Yulgong-ro

Junghakcheon-gil

1/4 mi

0.25 km

0

0

Area of detail

Namsan Park

Hongong

1 Changdeokgung 창덕궁
2 Jongmyo 종묘
3 Dalsaeneun Dalman Saengakhanda
  달세는 달만 생각한다
4 Insadong 인사동
5 Unyeonggung 운현궁
6 Jogyesa 조계사
7 Sanchon 산촌

Spend your second day exploring more of the historic heart of Seoul. The Jongno area is full of historic palaces and traditional arts, and even has a Buddhist temple. The palaces majestically sit among modern high-rises while auto and bus traffic speeds by. START: **Changdeokgung.**

Changdeokgung.

❶ ★★★ Changdeokgung. Originally built in 1405, this eastern palace has been rebuilt and renovated multiple times since. The grounds are divided into an administrative area, residential quarters, and the rear "secret garden," Biwon. English-language tours are at 10:30am and 2:30pm. Take the longer tour that includes the secret garden as well. ⏱ *80 min. 99 Yulgong-no, Jongno-gu.* ☎ *02/762-9513. www. eng.cdg.go.kr. Apr–Oct Tues–Sun 9am–6:30pm; Nov and Mar Tues–Sun 9am–5:30pm; Dec–Feb Tues–Sun 9am–5pm. Subway: Anguk, line 3 (exit 3) or Jongno 3(sam)-ga, line 6*

Tour the Palaces

The city of Seoul offers a combo ticket deal for visits to the main palaces. For just ₩10,000, you can get a ticket for Gyeonbokgung, Changdeokgung, Changgyeonggung, Deoksugung, and the royal shrine, Jongmyo. The combination ticket (which is good for a month) includes the longer, complete tour of Changdeokgung. It's a good deal, since the Changdeokgung/Biwon tour alone costs ₩5,000.

(exit 1 or 5). Bus: 109, 151, 162, 171, or 172. Map p 10.

❷ ★★★ **Jongmyo.** A place of worship for the kings of the Joseon Dynasty, this royal shrine was built by King Yi Sung-Gye, the first in the Joseon royal line, in 1394. Try to time your visit for the first Sunday of May for the impressive ceremony honoring the dead monarchs. At other times, the shrine's subtle architectural beauty can be best appreciated on an English-language guided tour at 10am, 11am, 2pm, or 3pm daily. Please call to make reservations in advance. ⏱ *1 hr. 1-2 Hunjeong-dong, Jongno-gu.* ☎ *02/ 765-0195. Admission ₩1,000 adults, W500 youth, free for seniors 65 and over and kids 6 and under. Mar–Oct Tues–Sun 9am–6pm; Nov–Feb Tues–Sun 9am–5:30pm. Subway: Jongno 3(sam)-ga, line 1 (exit 11) or line 3 or 5 (exit 8). Map p 10.*

③ ★★★ **Dalsaeneun Dalman Saengakhanda.** The name translates to "the moon bird only thinks of the moon." It's crowded with rustic objects and plants, but you can find a cozy corner. Enjoy one of the delicious teas that are good for you but taste like they aren't. *60 Gwan-hun-dong, Jongno-gu.* ☎ *02/720-6229. Daily 11am–11pm. $.*

❹ ★★★ **Insadong.** Although the historic arts district has gotten a bit touristy of late, there is still plenty to explore here. This is a great place to pick up Korean souvenirs to bring back home. They sell everything from notebooks made from *hanji* (traditional paper) as well as ceramics and calligraphic brushes. The area is best to explore on weekends, when the street is closed to vehicular traffic. ⏱ *1 hr. Subway: Anguk, line 3 (exit 6) or Jonggak, line 1 (exit 3). Bus: 109, 151, 162, 171, or 172. See p 35 for a detailed tour of the neighborhood.*

❺ ★★ **Unhyeongung.** The former home of Prince Gojong, it was converted into a palace later by his mother and his father, King Heung-seon. The king lived here for most of his life. A reenactment of the queen selection ceremony is held here every April, and occasional

May ceremony at Jongmyo.

Praying at Jogyesa.

reenactments of the royal wedding, "Garyeo," are also performed here. ⏱ *1 hr. 114-10 Unni-dong, Jongno-gu.* ☎ *02/766-9090. www.unhyeongung. or.kr. Admission ₩700 adults, ₩300 youths, free for seniors 65 and over and kids 12 and under. Apr–Oct 9am–7pm; Nov–Mar Tues–Sun 9am–6pm. Subway: Anguk, line 3 (exit 4) or Jongno 3(sam)-ga, line 5 (exit 4). Bus: 109, 151, 162, 171, or 172.*

6 Jogyesa. One of the few temples located in the middle of the city, Jogyesa is the center of Seon (aka Zen) Buddhism in Korea. If you want an English-language tour at anytime, make reservations in advance. A temple program (including a tea ceremony, basic mediation, a temple meal, and lotus lantern-making) is held every second and fourth Saturday for ₩20,000. ⏱ *30 min. 45 Gyeonji-dong, Jongno-gu.* ☎ *02/732-2183. www.jogyesa.org. Free admission. Jogyesa open daily 24 hr.; Dae-ungjeon (the main temple hall) and Geungnakjeon (smaller temple hall) daily 4am–9pm. Subway: Jonggak, line 1 (exit 2) or Anguk, line 3 (exit 2). Bus: 151, 172, 606, 1020, or 0015. Map p 10.*

7 ★★★ Sanchon. Run by a former Buddhist monk, the name of this restaurant means "mountain village." It serves temple cuisine, which is vegetarian, but the seasonal variety and flavors are a treat even for meat eaters. *Seungmu* (a Buddhist dance) is performed at 8 and 8:45pm every evening. It's located in a converted hanok up a winding alley in Insadong. *14 Gwan-hun-dong, Jongno-gu.* ☎ *02/735-0312. www.sanchon.com. $$$.*

A performance at Sanchon.

The Best in **Three Days**

The Best **Full-Day Tours**

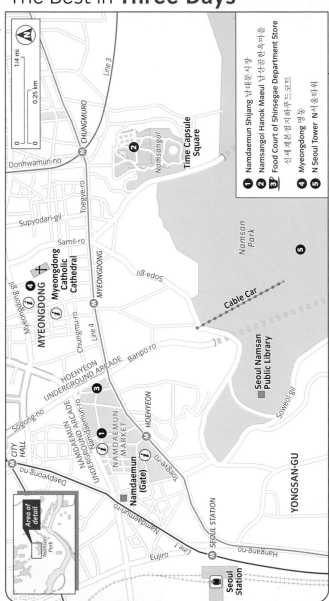

1. Namdaemun Shijang 남대문시장
2. Namsangol Hanok Maeul 남산골한옥마을
3. Food Court of Shinsegae Department Store 신세계본점지하푸드코트
4. Myeongdong 명동
5. N Seoul Tower N서울타워

Your third day is a great time to explore both the traditional and modern shopping districts. Even if you don't intend to buy anything, the hustle and bustle of the open markets is an exciting way to interact with Koreans. We've created an itinerary that includes both the fun of modern South Korea and the charms of the traditional culture. START: **Namdaemun Shijang.**

Namdaemun Shijang.

① ★★★ **Namdaemun Shijang.** The largest traditional market in the country used to be easily identified by the actual "Great South Gate" (that's what Namdaemun means), but it's now being renovated after being burned by an arsonist. Vendors hawk everything here from clothing to housewares. Don't be afraid to fend off aggressive sellers, and be prepared to bargain. The

rambling alleyways and tall buildings are also worth exploring. There are no set hours, but serious bargain hunters come for the wholesale night market (midnight–4am).
🕐 *1–2 hr. Open daily 24 hr. Subway: Hoehyeon, line 4 (exit 5).*

② kids **Namsangol Hanok Maeul.** Located at the northern foot of Namsan, this small village includes

Namsangol Hanok Maeul.

Shinsegae Department Store food court.

five restored traditional houses, called hanok. The houses range from those of peasants to royalty and give visitors insight into how Koreans used to live. ⏲ *1 hr. 84-1 Pil-dong 2(i)-ga, Jung-gu.* ☎ *02/2264-4412. Free admission. Apr–Oct 9am–9pm; Nov–Mar 9am–8pm. Subway: Chungmuro, line 3 or 4 (exit 3 or 4). Bus: 104, 105, 263, 371, or 400.*

3 ★★ **Food court of Shinsegae Department Store.** Some of the best values and variety of food options can be found on the basement level of the multistoried department stores that dot the city's landscape. Shinsegae's food court choices range from Indian curries to pizza, with a variety of Korean options as well. *52-5 Chungmuro 1(il)-ga, Jung-gu.* ☎ *02/1588-1234. $–$$.*

4 ★★★ **Myeongdong.** Cross the street from Shinsegae to enter the shopping district of Myeongdong. Although the street is most lively after dark, there are plenty of window-shopping opportunities anytime. The main streets feature designer brands and other better-known names, while bargains can be found at discount stores or street-cart vendors. The district extends from the Myeongdong subway station to the Lotte department store at Euljiro. It also has Korea's first Catholic cathedral. ⏲ *1½ hr. Hours vary, but most stores open daily 10am–10pm (until 11pm Fri and Sat). Subway: Myeongdong, line 4 (exit 5, 6, 7, or 8).* See p 43 for a detailed tour.

5 ★★★ **N Seoul Tower.** On top of Namsan ("South Mountain") sits this gleaming white tower, which offers some of the best views of the city. Try to arrive at sunset on a clear day to best enjoy the scenery. For a fancy meal, opt for N Grill; otherwise, there are plenty of affordable options in the lower-level food court. ⏲ *1 hr.* ☎ *02/3355-9277. www.nseoultower.co.kr. Hours vary, but often daily 10am–10pm. Bus: 2 (yellow) from Chungmuro Station (exit 2). Cable car: From Myeongdong Station (exit 3) walk 10 min. past Pacific Hotel to the cable car platform; ₩6,300 round-trip or ₩4,800 one-way adults, ₩4,000 round-trip or ₩3,000 one-way children.* ●

Historic Seoul

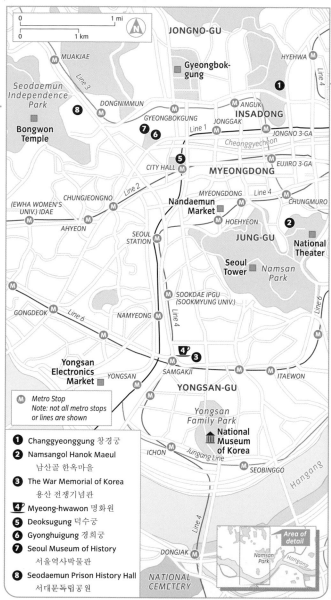

```
0                    1 mi
0          1 km
```

JONGNO-GU

MUAKJAE

Line 3

Gyeongbok-
gung

HYEHWA

Line 4

Seodaemun
Independence
Park

❽

DONGNIMMUN

GYEONGBOKGUNG

ANGUK

INSADONG

❶

Bongwon
Temple

❼ ❻

Line 1

JONGGAK

JONGNO 3-GA

Cheonggyecheon

EUJIRO 3-GA

❺

CITY HALL

MYEONGDONG

(EWHA WOMEN'S
UNIV.) IDAE

CHUNGJEONGNO

Line 2

MYEONGDONG

Line 4

CHUNGMURO

Nandaemun
Market

HOEHYEON

AHYEON

SEOUL
STATION

JUNG-GU

National
Theater

Seoul
Tower

*Namsan
Park*

❷

GONGDEOK

Line 6

NAMYEONG

SOOKDAE IPGU
(SOOKMYUNG UNIV.)

Line 4

Line 6

Yongsan
Electronics
Market

YONGSAN

SAMGAKJI

❹ ❸

YONGSAN-GU

ITAEWON

Ⓜ *Metro Stop*
*Note: not all metro stops
or lines are shown*

*Yongsan
Family Park*

🏛 National
Museum
of Korea

ICHON

Jungang Line

SEOBINGGO

Hangang

❶ Changgyeonggung 창경궁
❷ Namsangol Hanok Maeul
   남산골 한옥마을
❸ The War Memorial of Korea
   용산 전쟁기념관
❹ Myeong-hwawon 명화원
❺ Deoksugung 덕수궁
❻ Gyonghuigung 경희궁
❼ Seoul Museum of History
   서울역사박물관
❽ Seodaemun Prison History Hall
   서대문독립공원

DONGJAK

Line 4

*Area of
detail*

*Namsan
Park*

Hangang

NATIONAL
CEMETERY

Previous page: Junghwajeon building at Deoksugung.

It stands to reason that this over 600-year-old capital city would have a deep history. While most visitors see the main palaces and major museums, some of the smaller and lesser-known ones, tucked in among the towering office buildings, are worth visiting for further insight into the city's (and the country's) history. You barely have to scratch the surface to see that Seoul's roots run deep.

1 ★★ **Changgyeonggung.** Originally built by King Sejong, the fourth emperor of the Joseon Dynasty, this palace was a retirement gift for King Taejong. Often used as living quarters for queens and concubines, it was relocated and restored in 1983. ⏱ *1 hr. 2-1 Waryong-dong, Jongno-gu.* ☎ *02/762-4868. Admission ₩1,000 adults, ₩500 ages 7–18. Mar–Oct Tues–Fri 9am–6pm (until 7pm weekends and holidays); Nov–Feb Tues–Sun 9am–5:30pm. Subway: Hyehwa, line 4 (exit 4).*

2 kids ★ **Namsangol Hanok Maeul.** This small traditional village sits smack in the middle of the busiest part of the city. It has five restored houses, a pond, and hands-on traditional games for the kids to try. Performances are held here on holidays and select weekends. ⏱ *1 hr. 84-1 Pil-dong 2(i)-ga, Jung-gu.* ☎ *02/2264-4412. Free*

Changgyeonggung.

Korean War Memorial Museum.

admission. Apr–Oct Wed–Mon 9am–9pm; Nov–Mar Wed–Mon 9am–8pm. Subway: Chungmuro, line 3 or 4 (exit 3 or 4).

3 ★★ **The War Memorial of Korea.** Once the headquarters of the Korean infantry, this monument and museum not only memorializes

Daily commemorative ceremony at Deoksugung.

the Korean War (which is a big part of the museum's displays), but also war in general. More fascinating than you would expect, although you can give a miss to the silly "war experience room." 🕐 1½ hr. Yong-san-dong 1(il)-ga, Yongsan-gu. ☎ 02/709-3139. www.warmemo. or.kr. Tues–Sun 9am–6pm. Subway: Samgakji, line 4 or 6 (exit 12).

4 Myeong-hwawon. Very close to the War Memorial, this restaurant specializes in Korean-style Chinese food. You can choose from jjamp-pong (spicy seafood noodle soup), goon mandu (fried dumplings), or tangsuyeok (sweet and sour pork). 14-28 Hangang-ro 1(il)-ga, Yongsan-gu. ☎ 02/792-2969. Closed daily 3:30–5:30pm. $–$$.

Seoul Museum of History.

5 ★ **Deoksugung.** Known for its stone wall and its wide bridge, this structure was built by King Wolsan, but not used as a palace until King Gwanghae took power in 1611. The first Western-style building in Seoul, the Junghwajeon still has a secret passageway to the Russian Emissary. 🕐 1½ hr. 5-1 Jeong-dong, Jung-gu. ☎ 02/771-9952. www.deoksugung. go.kr. Admission ₩1,000 adults, ₩500 ages 7–18, free for seniors and kids age 6 and under. Tues–Sun 9am–10pm. Subway: City Hall, line 11 (exit 2) or line 12 (exit 12).

6 ★ **Gyeonghuigung.** This "Pal-ace of the West" was the secondary home to the king during the latter half of the Joseon Dynasty. It used to have an arched bridge that con-nected it to **Deoksugung** (see above). A shadow of its former splen-dor (its original front gate is the Silla Hotel's entrance), its architecture still tells of a different time when the mountains and the direction of the sun meant something. 🕐 30 min. 1 Sinmunno 2(i)-ga, Jongno-gu. ☎ 02/724-0274. Free admission. Mon–Fri 9am–6pm; Sat–Sun 10am–6pm. Sub-way: Seodaemun, line 5 (exit 4).

7 kids ★ **Seoul Museum of History.** Although some of this museum's displays provide insight

The Joseon Dynasty

Started by King Taejo Yi Seong-gye, the royal Yi family governed Korea for five centuries (1392–1897, to be exact). Marking the last imperial rulers of the peninsula, it was the longest running Confucian dynasty in history. Its 500-plus years were not peaceful ones, however. Invasions from Japan, China, and Manchuria caused the peninsula to enact harsh isolationist policies, during which it was given its nickname, "The Hermit Kingdom," when it enjoyed nearly 200 years of peace. By the end of the 19th century, however, the dynasty's power had waned, and the Japanese took it over as the "Korean Empire" when it signed the Treaty of Shimonoseki after the First Sino-Japanese War. The rest, as they say, is history.

into the city's history, the paucity of English labels makes it less useful. It's still worth a visit to view old maps and the miniature scale model of the sprawling city. 🕐 *1 hr. 2-1 Sinmunno 2(i)-ga, Jongno-gu.* ☎ *02/724-0194. www.museum.seoul.kr. Admission ₩700 ages 20–64. Mar–Oct Tues–Fri 9am–10pm, Sat–Sun 10am–7pm; Nov–Feb Tues–Fri 9am–9pm, Sat–Sun 10am–6pm. Located right next to Gyeonghuigung.*

⑧ Seodaemun Prison History Hall.

This prison-cum-museum was originally built at the end of the Joseon Dynasty and used as a place to torture and kill Korean patriots during the Japanese occupation. Note that displays are not in English. *101 Hyeonjeo-dong, Seodaemun-gu.* ☎ *02/363-9750. www.sscmc.or.kr. Admission ₩1,500 adults, ₩1,000 teens, ₩500 children. Mar–Oct Tues–Sun 9:30am–6pm; Nov–Feb Tues–Sun 9:30am–5pm. Subway: Dongnimmun, line 3 (exit 5). About a 15-min. walk from Gyeonghuigung.*

Seodaemun Prison History Hall.

Seoul with Kids

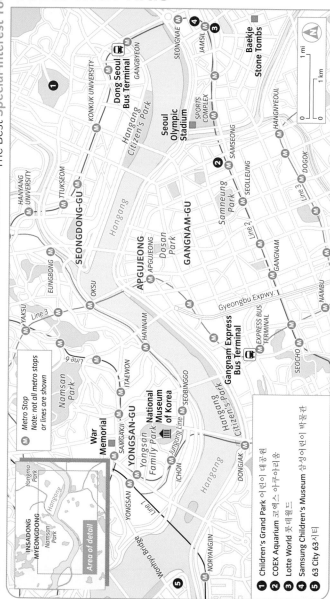

1 Children's Grand Park 어린이 대공원
2 COEX Aquarium 코엑스 아쿠아리움
3 Lotte World 롯데월드
4 Samsung Children's Museum 삼성어린이 박물관
5 63 City 63시티

Metro Stop
Note: not all metro stops
or lines are shown

Dong Seoul
Bus Terminal

Seoul
Olympic
Stadium

Baekje
Stone Tombs

Gangnam Express
Bus Terminal

War
Memorial

National
Family Park Museum
of Korea

Area of detail

INSADONG
MYEONGDONG

Seoul may not seem like the most child-friendly city at first glance, but there's plenty here to keep the little ones amused. A trip to an amusement park, like Lotte World or the Children's Grand Park, can take a whole day. Take the kids for an afternoon in the COEX Mall or even just a run around one of the many parks in the city. If you happen to visit in the spring, there's even a public holiday dedicated to them on May 5. It's great for the kids, but it also means that child-friendly attractions are extra crowded. If you have the time, take the family on a day trip to **Suwon** (p 143) for a trip to **Everland** (p 144, another amusement park with more rides than Lotte World) and a visit to the **Korean Folk Village** (p 144).

❶ ★★★ **Children's Grand Park.** A huge complex, this family park includes hiking trails, a botanical garden, a zoo, a small amusement park with rides good for smaller children, and an outdoor stage. Over half of the area is green space, perfect for kids to run around. *18 Neung-dong, Gwangjin-gu. ☎ 02/450-9311. www.children park.or.kr. Zoo ₩6,000 adults, ₩4,500 teens and children. Admission to Character World and other amusements vary. Daily 5am–10pm (zoo and gardens 11am–5pm, until 4pm Nov–Mar). Subway : Children's Grand Park, line 7 (exit 1).*

Baboon at Children's Grand Park.

❷ ★ **COEX Aquarium.** Inside the **COEX Mall** (p 68), the aquarium with its "Undersea Tunnel" and thousands of fish is a fun draw for the kids. Over 600 species of underwater creatures are on view, as well as sea otters and polar bears. Try to time your visit for morning shark feeding time. *159*

COEX Mall Aquarium.

Samsung Children's Museum.

Samseong-dong, Gangnam-gu. ☎ 02/6002-6200. www.coexaqua. co.kr. Admission ₩17,500 adults, ₩14,500 teens, ₩11,000 children, kids 4 and under. Daily 10am–8pm (last entry 7pm). Subway: Samseong, line 2 (exit 5 or 6).

3 ★★ **Lotte World.** Not only does this complex include the world's largest indoor amusement park (Adventure Land) and the less impressive outdoor park (Magic Island), but it also has a hotel, a department store, a swimming pool, a bowling alley, a shooting range, movie theaters, and an ice rink. Go early on weekdays to avoid the crowds. The best meal bargains are found in the food court. *40-1 Jamsil-dong, Songpa-gu.* ☎ *02/411-2000. www.lotteworld.com. Admission ₩26,000 adults, ₩23,000 teens, ₩20,000 children; slightly cheaper after 4pm. Subway: Jamsil, line 2 or 8 (exit 4).*

4 ★★★ **Samsung Children's Museum.** Best for kids 12 and under, this museum is designed with education and experience in mind. There are plenty of hands-on exploration possibilities for even toddlers. *7-26 Sincheon-dong, Songpa-gu.* ☎ *02/2143-3600.*

Tips for Traveling with Kids

They're adding more and more elevators and escalators to Seoul's subway stations, but not all of them have them yet. Strollers are difficult to maneuver on the stairs, so you may wish to take a taxi or bus when traveling with toddlers (although kind strangers always seem to be helping mothers in distress). Kids 7 and under can ride the buses and subways for free when accompanied by an adult (one child free per adult) and children 4 and under get to ride the trains for free (children ages 4 to 13 get a 50% discount). Strollers are available (sometimes for free) at amusement parks, national museums, department stores, and mega discount marts. Large department stores and amusement parks usually have nursing facilities next to the restrooms. Also remember that most traditional Korean restaurants will only have chopsticks and spoons, so you may wish to pack a portable fork before your trip.

Lotte World.

http://kids.samsungfoundation.org/
eng. Admission ₩5,000 ages 12 and
over, ₩6,000 ages 3–11, ₩3,000
ages 1–2. Tues–Sun 10am–6pm (last
entry 4pm). Subway: Jamsil, line 2
(exit 8) or line 8 (exit 9). Bus: 3216,
3313, 3315, 3413, or 3414.

⑤ ★★ **63 City.** Though not the
tallest building in the city anymore,
this is still a fun place to bring your
family. The sea lion show and the
African penguins are highlights at
the **Sea World** aquarium; the IMAX
theatre has shows in three languages; the wax museum provides
photo ops with Beethoven, Jesus,
Picasso, and Korean celebrities. *For
more info, see p 118. 60 Yeouido-
dong, Yeongdeungpo-gu.* ☎ *02/789-
5679. Admission prices vary.
Subway: Yeouinaru, line 5 (exit 4);
then take free shuttle.*

63 Building.

Relax & Rejuvenate in Seoul

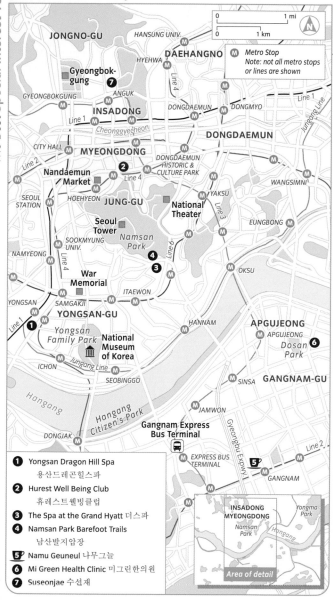

JONGNO-GU

HANSUNG UNIV.

DAEHANGNO

HYEHWA

Line 4

0   1 mi
0   1 km

Ⓜ Metro Stop
Note: not all metro stops
or lines are shown

Gyeongbok-gung ⑦

GYEONGBOKGUNG

ANGUK

INSADONG

Line 1

DONGDAEMUN

DONGMYO

Line 1

Jungang Line

Cheonggyecheon

CITY HALL

MYEONGDONG

DONGDAEMUN

Line 2

DONGDAEMUN HISTORIC & CULTURE PARK

Nandaemun Market ②

Line 4

WANGSIMNI

SEOUL STATION

HOEHYEON

JUNG-GU

YAKSU

National Theater

Line 3

EUNGBONG

Seoul Tower

SOOKMYUNG UNIV.

Namsan Park

Line 6

NAMYEONG

Line 4

④

③

OKSU

War Memorial

ITAEWON

YONGSAN

SAMGAKJI

YONGSAN-GU

HANNAM

APGUJEONG

APGUJEONG

Ⓜ

①

Yongsan Family Park

National Museum of Korea

Dosan Park

⑥

ICHON

Jungang Line

SEOBINGGO

SINSA

GANGNAM-GU

Hangang

JAMWON

Hangang Citizen's Park

Gangnam Express Bus Terminal

Gyeongbu EXPWY

DONGJAK

EXPRESS BUS TERMINAL

⑤

Line 2

GANGNAM

INSADONG MYEONGDONG

Namsan Park

Hangang

Yongma Park

Area of detail

① Yongsan Dragon Hill Spa
용산드래곤힐스파

② Hurest Well Being Club
휴레스트웰빙클럽

③ The Spa at the Grand Hyatt 더스파

④ Namsan Park Barefoot Trails
남산발지압장

⑤ Namu Geuneul 나무그늘

⑥ Mi Green Health Clinic 미그린한의원

⑦ Suseonjae 수선재

Seoul may be busy and frenzied, but it's also a great place for balance and slowing down. South Koreans take their leisure time seriously, maybe because most people get only one day off a week. If soaking in a group bath isn't your idea of fun, there are plenty of other options to get your relaxation on.

❶ ★ Yongsan Dragon Hill Spa. One of the fanciest *jjimjilbang* ("steam rooms") in the city, this Chinese dragon-themed spa includes a swimming pool and health center, in addition to the steam rooms and baths. *40-713 Hangang-no 3(sam)-ga, Yongsan-gu. www.dragonhillspa. co.kr. ☎ 02/792-0002. Admission ₩10,000 5am–8pm, ₩12,000 8pm–5am. Open daily 24 hr. Subway: Yongsan (exit 1) or Sinyongsan, line 4 (exit 4).*

❷ ★ Hurest Well Being Club. Spanning the 15th through 17th floors of the Myeongdong Tower is this popular jjimjilbang, a great place to soak away your aches and pains and leave your worries behind in the hot waters. *31-1 Myeongdong 2(i)-ga, Jung-gu. ☎ 02/778-8307. Admission ₩10,000 5am–9pm, ₩12,000 9pm–5am. Open daily 24 hr. Subway: Myeongdong, line 4 (exit 5).*

❸ ★★ The Spa at the Grand Hyatt. Come here to experience a blend of Korean and European spa techniques, like a deep-tissue massage with ginseng, a facial with lavender and tea tree oil, or a Turkish salt body polish, in a calming setting. *747-7 Hannam 2(i)-dong, Yongsan-gu. ☎ 02/797-1234. www.seoul. grand.hyatt.com. 60-min treatments ₩150,000 and up. Subway: Noksapyeong, line 6 (exit 1); cross the road and take bus no. 3. Bus: No. 402 from Seoul Station.*

Yongsan Dragon Hill Spa.

The Spa at the Grand Hyatt.

4 Namsan Park Barefoot Trails. Cobblestone paths are found all over Seoul. Based on reflexology and Oriental medicine, the foot paths are said to improve blood circulation and activate internal organ functions. It's also nice for tired feet. *Next to the Namsan Outdoor Botanic Garden (walking distance from the Grand Hyatt).*

5 Namu Geuneul. For a totally different experience, get an underwater pedicure at the "Tree Shade" cafe. For a small fee, tiny fish nibble the dead skin from your feet. A selection of coffee, teas, and a dessert buffet adds to the fun. Check the website for other locations. *2F, BSX Bldg. (across from the CGV Gangnam), Gangnam-gu. ☎ 02/1644-2633. www.restree.net (Korean only). Subway: Gangnam, line 2 (exit 6). $.*

Korean Bathhouses

Korean bathhouses are segregated by gender, which is good since you'll be walking around in your birthday suit in front of strangers, all in their own birthday suits. You will be given a locker key for your shoes and belongings (sometimes a separate locker for just your shoes at the entryway). Be sure to wear your key around your ankle or wrist so you don't lose it. You should then take off everything (including jewelry and watches) and head for the shower facilities. Everyone is expected to wash completely before going into the communal bath. They'll provide shampoo, shower gel, clean towels, brushes, lotion, hair dryers, and even hair spray, if you've forgotten yours. After a good soaking, most Koreans scrub themselves raw with a scratchy towel that feels like a cat's tongue. You can also try one of the dry or wet saunas, or cool down in the cold bath. There is no time limit, so soak, scrub, and linger as long as you'd like. Most jjimjilbang are open 24/7, so you can even sleep in a large communal room—that is, if you don't mind sleeping in a large room full of snoring strangers.

6 ★ **Mi Green Health Clinic.**
Don't be put off by the hospital-like setting, since this clinic is known for its Oriental medicine and holistic approach to skin care. The *makge-olli* (milky rice wine) massage is top-notch, but their facials are what bring in the regulars. *2F, 665-6 Sinsa-dong, Gangnam-gu. ☎ 02/548-3333. www.mi-green.co.kr (Korean only). Mon, Tues, Thurs, and Fri 11am–9pm; Sat 10am–4pm. Subway: Apgujeong, line 3 (exit 3).*

7 ★★ **Suseonjae.** *Seon-gye* is a certain type of Korean meditation, derived from an ancient meditation practice called "seondo." Its followers created this society to practice and teach this type of meditation. Various classes and programs are available. *86 Gwanhun-dong, Jongno-gu. ☎ 02/722-1108. www.suseonjae.org. Classes ₩15,000 and up. Subway: Anguk, line 3 (exit 6).*

Namsan Park Barefoot Trails.

Gastronomic Seoul

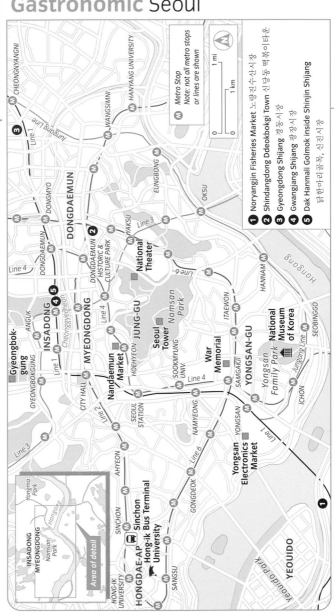

Metro Stop
Note: not all metro stops
or lines are shown

1 mi

1 km

1 Noryangjin Fisheries Market 노량진수산시장
2 Shindangdong Ddeokbokgi Town 신당동 떡볶이타운
3 Gyeongdong Shijang 경동시장
4 Gwangjang Shijang 광장시장
5 Dak Hanmali Golmok inside Shinjin Shijang
닭한마리골목, 신진시장

ood options are endless in this sprawling city. Choices range from ₩1,000 treats from street carts to multicourse extravaganzas by celebrity chefs, and everything in between. We've compiled a listing of open markets, "let's eat alleys" (*mokja golmok*), and areas known for special dishes to guide you on a foodie's tour. Our individual restaurant recommendations can be found in chapter 6, "The Best Dining," where you'll find tiny hole-in-the-wall noodle joints, fancy bakeries, barbecue restaurants, and anything your heart (and stomach) desires.

❶ ★★★ **Noryangjin Fisheries Market.** Early risers can check out the auction at this lively wholesale market at dawn. Browse among the burbling tanks full of octopus, crab, shrimp, clams, and more. Then take your purchase upstairs to have the vendors slice the fresh sashimi (*hwae*) straight from the water onto your plate. They'll take the bones and make it into a spicy hot pot (*maeuntang*) for a few won more. Or you can just have them grill the fish with just a bit of salt and they'll serve it with rice and other side dishes. *13-8 Noryangjin-dong, Dong-jak-gu.* ☎ *02/815-2000. www.susansijang.co.kr. Wholesale market daily 2am–6pm. Raw-fish market open daily 24 hr. Subway: Noryangjin, line 1 (exit 1).*

Noryangjin Fisheries Market.

❷ **Shindangdong Ddeok-bokgi Town.** The name sounds fancier than it really is—a street lined with *ddeokbokgi* (rice sticks)

restaurants on either side. For ₩10,000, you'll get a huge pan of rice cakes, ramen, spicy sauce, and fish cakes, enough to share with a hungry friend. They have a ddeok-bokgi street festival here every September or October. *Shingdang 1(il)-dong, Jung-gu. Closed Sun. Subway: Cheongguk, line 5 (exit 1).*

Shindangdong Ddeokbokgi Town.

Flatcakes at Gwangjang Shijang.

④ ★★★ Gwangjang Shijang. The "let's eat alley" at this market known for its fabric selection is one of the best-kept secrets in Seoul. Get *nokdu buchingae* (mungbean flatcakes) larger than your face for a mere ₩5,000, or just point and eat from any number of Korean dishes made fresh. This is Seoul's idea of an "open kitchen," at a ridiculously affordable price. *6-1 Yeji-dong, Jongno-gu.* ☎ *02/2267-0291. www. kwangjangmarket.co.kr (Korean only). Mon–Sat 7am–7pm. Subway: Jongno 5(o)-ga, line 1 (exit 8).*

⑤ ★ Dak Hanmali Golmok. The name translates to "One Chicken Alley," and you'll find plenty of restaurants cooking those birds. Put the whole chicken in the broth and cut with scissors. Choose side items like rice cakes and potatoes. Prepare the accompanying sauce and enjoy. Then order some *kal guksu* (hand-cut noodles) to enjoy with the remaining broth. This hidden food alley is also known for all the fresh fish grilled outside on the open fire. *Inside Shinjin Shijang (across from Pyeonghwa Shijang), Dongdaemun-gu. Subway: Jongno 5(o)-ga, line 1 (exit 5). Or walk toward Dongdaemun from Gwangjang Shijang.* ●

③ ★★ Gyeongdong Shijang. What started as an impromptu gathering of farmers on a fallow field after the Korean War has become one of the country's largest Oriental medicine markets. It also spills into one of the last "traditional" food markets in Seoul—visit it soon before they modernize it. *Jegi-dong, Dongdaemun-gu.* ☎ *02/967-8721. www.kyungdong mart.com (Korean only). Oriental medicine market daily 9am–7pm. Traditional market daily 4am–7pm. Subway: Jegi, line 1 (exit 2).*

Cooking fish on the outdoor grills at Dak Hanmali Golmok.

Insadong

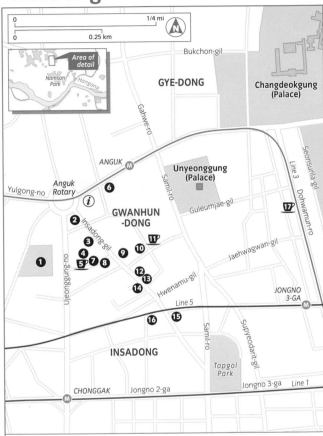

1/4 mi
0.25 km

Bukchon-gil

GYE-DONG

Changdeokgung (Palace)

Area of detail

Namsan Park

Hangang

Gahwer-ro

Seonsunla-gil

Dohwamun-ro

ANGUK Ⓜ

Samil-ro

Unyeonggung (Palace)

Yulgong-no

Anguk Rotary

ⓘ

GWANHUN -DONG

Guleumjae-gil

17

❷

Insadong-gil

❻

Jaehwagwan-gil

JONGNO 3-GA Ⓜ

❸

❹

❺

❼

❽

❾

11

10

12

13

14

Hwenamu-gil

Line 5

Ujeongguk-ro

❶

16

15

Samil-ro

Supyeodarit-gil

INSADONG

Tapgol Park

CHONGGAK Ⓜ

Jongno 2-ga

Jongno 3-ga   Line 1

---

❶ Jogyesa 조계사

❷ Tongmunkwan 통문관

❸ Toto's Nostalgia Museum
& Gift Shop 토토의 오래된 물건

❹ Korean Craft & Design Foundation
한국공예디자인문화진흥원

❺ Yetchatjip 옛찻집

❻ Mokin Museum 목인박물관

❼ Kwanhoon Gallery 관훈갤러리

❽ Knife Gallery 칼 박물관

❾ Ssamziegil 쌈지길

❿ Kyung-in Museum of Fine Art
경인미술관

⓫ Mingadaheon (Min's Club) 민가다헌

⓬ Insa Art Plaza 인사아트플라자

⓭ Tong-in Store 통인화랑

⓮ Gukje Embroidery 국제자수원

⓯ Bongwon Calligraphy 봉원필방

⓰ Beautiful Tea Museum
오설록녹차박물관

⓱ Rice Cake Tteok Museum 떡박물관

Previous page: Lanterns at Seongnagwon.

Insadong has been the city's center of arts and culture since the Joseon Dynasty. Although chain stores like Starbucks and modern shops have begun to spring up on the main street, Insadong-gil, beyond the modern facades you'll find antique shops, art galleries, and *hanok* (traditional houses) converted to teahouses. This tour lets you explore the winding alleyways and multistoried complexes to find secret art shops and quiet corners. **START: Anguk Station, line 3 (exit 6).**

Toto's Nostalgia Museum and Giftshop.

① **Jogyesa.** Start here at this small temple tucked away in the middle of the busy city. *See p ###.*

② **Tongmunkwan.** Selling antique books since 1934, the shop is run by the original owner's grandson. The door is always closed (the owner is afraid of visitors damaging some of the century-old tomes), but it's worth venturing in to see history bound in now-fading pages. ⏱ *15 min. 147 Gwanhun-dong, Jongno-gu.* ☎ *02/734-4092. www.tongmunkwan.co.kr. Closed Sun.*

③ kids **★★ Toto's Nostalgia Museum and Giftshop.** This tiny storefront and "museum" is jam-packed with Korean nostalgia— toys, robots, dolls, schoolbooks, and other ephemera from the 1960s to the 1980s. ⏱ *30 min. 2F, 169-2 Gwanhun-dong, Jongno-gu.* ☎ *02/725-1756. Admission ₩1,000.*

④ **★ Korean Craft & Design Foundation.** Don't let the official-sounding name put you off this high-quality souvenir shop. Stamped with the UNESCO seal of excellence, you'll get the real deal made by Korea's living treasures. ⏱ *30 min. 182-2 Gwanhun-dong, Jongno-gu.* ☎ *02/733-9041. www.kcdf.kr.*

⑤ **★★★ Yetchatjip.** Duck into a tiny alley to find the oldest teahouse in Insadong. This converted hanok opens into a wonderful garden perfect for enjoying a traditional cup. The resident parrots occasionally squawk out in Korean. *2F, 196-5 Gwanhun-dong, Jongno-gu.* ☎ *02/722-5332. $.*

⑥ **★★ Mokin Museum.** A museum dedicated to wooden

Insa Art Plaza.

totems of animals and figures. Don't miss the rooftop teashop/sculpture garden. *1hr. 83 Gyeonji-dong, Jongno-gu. ☎ 02/722-5332. www.mokinmuseum.com (Korean only). Admission ₩5,000.*

❼ **Kwanhoon Gallery.** The first gallery in Seoul to exhibit modern art, it has launched many a Korean artist's career. *30 min. 195 Gwanhun-dong, Jongno-gu. ☎ 02/733-6469. http://kwanhoongallery.com.*

❽ **Knife Gallery.** Just as the name suggests, this gallery showcases and sells hundreds of knives of many persuasions. *30 min. 192-11 Gwanhun-dong, Jongno-gu. ☎ 02/735-4431. www.knifegallery.co.kr.*

Insadong-gil, Insadong's bustling main drag.

❾ ★★★ **Ssamziegil.** Designed by artists to showcase their wares, this multistoried complex is a wonderful way to discover artists, traditional shops, modern design studios, and other exhibits. You may be lucky and chance upon one of many arts events held here. *1 hr. 38 Gwanhun-dong, Jongno-gu. ☎ 02/736-0088.*

❿ ★★★ **Kyung-in Museum of Fine Art.** This converted hanok is now a gallery complex with exhibit spaces, an outdoor stage, an arts and crafts shop, and a fabulous courtyard teahouse, Dawon. *1 hr. 30-1 Gwanhun-dong, Jongno-gu. ☎ 02/733-4448. www.kyunginart.co.kr.*

11 ★★★ **Mingadaheon (Min's Club).** Korean fusion food is served in this gorgeously restored hanok. The huge wine list is as much as a surprise as the inventive dishes. *66-7 Gyeongun-dong, Jongno-gu. ☎ 02/723-2966. $$$.*

⓬ ★★ **Insa Art Plaza.** A giant art mall that's great for picking up souvenirs made of *hanji* (traditional paper) and other folk crafts. The basement level sells Korean fast food. ⏱ *1 hr. 22 Gwanhun-dong, Jongno-gu.* ☎ *02/733-9419.*

⓭ ★★ **Tong-in Store.** Although it began as an antiques store more than 85 years ago, it has expanded to include modern pieces in its collection. Explore all the floors to see a wide expanse of Korean furniture and ceramics. ⏱ *30 min. 16 Gwanhun-dong, Jongno-gu.* ☎ *02/733-4867.*

⓮ **Gukje Embroidery.** Since the late '70s, each ornament, quilt, or other colorful piece here has been hand-embroidered in the traditional style. ⏱ *30 min. 197-28 Gwanhun-dong, Jongno-gu.* ☎ *02/723-0830.*

⓯ **Bongwon Calligraphy.** For more than 3 decades, artists have been buying the inkstones and hanji at this calligraphic supply store. ⏱ *15 min. 27 Insadong, Jongno-gu.* ☎ *02/739-9611.*

⓰ **Beautiful Tea Museum.** A good place to buy the latest works of up-and-coming Korean ceramicists and Chinese and Tibetan artists, it also serves more than 100

Beautiful Tea Museum.

different teas in a hanok garden. ⏱ *30 min. 193-1 Insadong, Jongno-gu.* ☎ *02/735-6678.*

⓱ ★ **Rice Cake (Tteok) Museum.** This museum and educational institute also doubles as a rice cake cafe. Snack on a selection of meticulously presented rice cakes or just stop for a traditional tea. ₩3,000 admission to the museum. *164-2 Waryeong-dong, Jongno-gu.* ☎ *02/741-5447. www.tkmuseum.or.kr. $.*

Rice Cake Museum.

Samcheong-dong and **Bukchon**

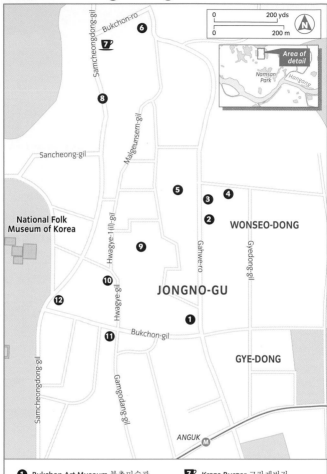

0   200 yds
0   200 m

Area of detail

Namsan Park   Hangang

Samcheongdong-gil

Bukchon-ro

Sancheong-gil

Malgeunsem-gil

National Folk Museum of Korea

WONSEO-DONG

Gahwe-ro

Gyedong-gil

Hwagye-1(il)-gil

JONGNO-GU

Hwagye-gil

Bukchon-gil

GYE-DONG

Samcheongdong-gil

Gamgodang-gil

ANGUK Ⓜ

1 Bukchon Art Museum 북촌미술관
2 Gahoe Museum 가회박물관
3 Seoul Museum of Chicken Art
    서울닭문화관
4 Hansangsoo Embroidery Museum
    한상수자수박물관
5 Bukchon Hanok Maeul 북촌 한옥마을
6 Owl Art & Craft Museum
    부엉이미술공예박물관

7 Kraze Burger 크라제버거
8 Samcheongdong-gil 삼청동길
9 Jeongdok Library 정독도서관
10 World Jewellery Museum
    세계장신구박물관
11 Art Sonje Center 아트선재센터
12 Kukje Gallery 국제갤러리

I t wasn't until the past decade that the city's government allowed development in Samcheong-dong. And develop they did. Still, the people who renovated the hanok into restaurants, cafes, and galleries retained the comfortable flair of the traditional architecture while adding whimsical touches. Neighboring Samcheong-dong's main street, the Bukchon Hanok Maeul offers a purer look at older architecture. Put on your walking shoes to visit a quiet neighborhood climbing the hill overlooking the sprawling city below. START: **Anguk Station, line 3 (exit 3).**

❶ ★ Bukchon Art Museum.
You can't miss the sculpture of two heads devouring a bench in front of this large museum. It exhibits both contemporary and traditional art from Korea, China, and beyond.
🕐 *1 hr. 170-4 Gahoe-dong, Jongno-gu. ☎ 02/741-2296. www.bukchon artmuseum.com. Admission ₩2,000 adults, ₩1,000 ages 7–18. Tues–Sun 11am–6pm.*

❷ kids ★ Gahoe Museum. This small museum (housed in a converted hanok) exhibits paintings, amulets, and other items from Korea's not-so-distant folk roots. Guided tours in English available Tuesday to Friday. 🕐 *1hr. 11-103 Gahoe-dong, Jongno-gu. ☎ 02/741-0466. Admission ₩3,000 adults ₩2,000 ages 18 and under. Tues–Sun 10am–6pm.*

Visitor Tip

Stop by the **Tourist Info Center** just north of Anguk Station to get the Bukchon Museum Freedom pass for ₩10,000, which is good for admission to the Gahoe Museum, Hansangsoo Embroidery Museum, Dong-Lim Museum, Museum of Korean Buddhist Art, and Seoul Museum of Chicken Art. It can be purchased at any one of those museums as well.

❸ kids Seoul Museum of Chicken Art. As the name suggests, this private space is dedicated to all things chicken. The first floor houses the permanent collection and a cafe, while the second-floor exhibit changes with the

Gahoe Museum.

Seoul Museum of Chicken Art.

❹ ★ Hansangsoo Embroidery Museum. This small museum is dedicated to art of traditional embroidery, mostly by Han Sang-soo, who is has been deemed "Intangible Cultural Asset #80." The best part is trying your hand at embroidering a handkerchief. Instruction is available for only ₩3,000, but only in Korean. ⏱ *30 min. 11-32 Gahoe-dong, Jongno-gu.* ☎ *02/744-1545. www.hansangsoo. com (mostly Korean). Admission ₩3,000 adults ₩2,000 ages 18 and under. Tues–Sun 10am–5pm.*

❺ ★★★ Bukchon Hanok Maeul. Once a village for the city's aristocrats, it is now a preserved neighborhood with tiled-roofed homes dating back nearly 600 years to the Joseon Dynasty. No official tour of the area is available, but you can pick up a map at the Tourist Info Center (just north of Anguk Station) and take a leisurely walk around the houses to see traditional homes and the view of the city from the hillside. Be prepared for an uphill walk through the narrow alleyways. ⏱ *2 hr. Gahoe-dong, Jongno-gu.*

seasons. ⏱ *30 min. 12 Gahoe-dong, Jongno-gu.* ☎ *02/763-9995. www. kokodac.com (Korean only). Admission ₩3,000 adults ₩2,000 children. Tues–Sat 10am–6pm.*

Bukchon Hanok Maeul.

A painting at Kukje Gallery.

☎ 02/3707-8270. http://bukchon. seoul.go.kr. Free.

6 kids ★ **Owl Art & Craft Museum.** One woman's 40-year-old obsession is viewable in this tiny museum. She'll even serve you tea from her owl mug collection. ⏱ 30 min. 27-21 Samcheong-dong, Jongno-gu. ☎ 02/3210-2902. www.owlmuseum.co.kr (mostly Korean). Admission ₩5,000 adults, ₩4,000 ages 13–18, ₩3,000 ages 3 to 12. Thurs–Sun 10am–7pm (until 6pm in winter).

7 **Kraze Burger.** This ubiquitous Korean chain is a dependable place for a quick burger and fries before continuing your Samcheong-dong adventure. 35-251 Samcheong-dong, Jongno-gu. ☎ 02/3147-1536. www. kraze.co.kr. $.

8 ★★ **Samcheongdong-gil.** Make your way down the main drag and check out the funky cafes and restaurants that line both sides of the street. ⏱ 1 hr.

9 ★ **Jeongdok Library.** At the former site of the Gyeonggi High School, this building was converted to a public library in 1977. The grounds are nice to stroll through when the cherry blossoms are in bloom in the spring or when the

ginkgo trees turn yellow in autumn. ⏱ 1 hr. 2 Hwa-dong, Jongno-gu. ☎ 02/2011-5799. Free. http://211.61. 24.181/english. General reading room open Mon–Fri 7am–11pm (Mar–Oct), 8am–11pm (Nov–Feb), Sat–Sun closes 10pm. Closed 1st and 3rd Wed of every month.

10 ★ **World Jewellery Museum.** A glittering 30-year-old collection from the wife of a former diplomat. Jewels, sculptures and other artifacts gathered from around the world fill two floors. ⏱ 30 min. 75-3 Hwa-dong, Jongno-gu. ☎ 02/ 730-1610. www.wjmuseum.com. Admission ₩7,000 adults, ₩5,000 students. Wed–Sun 11am–5pm.

11 ★★ **Art Sonje Center.** An art complex in the area, it's well known for its occasional performances and exhibits of cutting-edge Korean and international artists. ⏱ 30 min. 144-2 Sogyeok-dong, Jongno-gu. ☎ 02/733-8945. www.artsonje.org. Admission ₩3,000. Tues–Sun 11am–7pm.

12 **Kukje Gallery.** This small gallery exhibits works by well-known Korean and international artists. Past shows have showcased Bill Viola, Louise Bourgeois, Joan Mitchell, and Eva Hesse. ⏱ 15 min. 59-1 Sogyeok-dong, Jongno-gu. ☎ 02/735-8449. www.kukje.com. Free. Mon–Sat 10am–5pm, Sun and holidays 10am–5pm.

Myeongdong

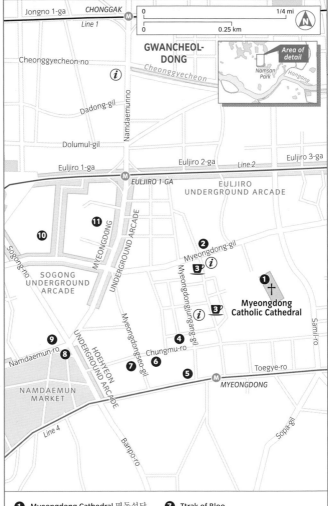

1. Myeongdong Cathedral 명동성당
2. ABC Mart ABC마트
3. Myeongdong Gyoja 명동교자
4. Codes Combine 코데즈 컴바인
5. Migliore 밀레오레
6. SPAO 스파오
7. Ttrak of Bloo
8. Shinsegae Department Store 신세계백화점
9. Bank of Korea Museum 화폐금융박물관
10. Wongudan Altar 원구단
11. Lotte Department Store 롯데백화점

If you love to shop and eat, Myeongdong is the place to be. Department stores open in the morning, but the real fun and action happens after the sun goes down. Most of the major brands can be found here, but the real bargain hunting can be found at the street carts and smaller shops tucked in between the big names. Look beyond the modern shops and restaurants to see reminders of Seoul's complicated history. START: **Myeongdong Station, line 4 (exit 8).**

❶ ★★ Myeongdong Cathedral. The first and main Catholic church in the country was built on the grounds where Korean Catholics have gathered since 1784. (The building was finished in 1898.) This Gothic revival building is not only a landmark in the area, but also a shrine for the Korean martyrs—believers who were violently killed when Christians (and Catholics in particular) were heavily persecuted during the Joseon period. ⏱ *30 min. 1-8 Myeongdong 2(i)-ga, Jung-gu.* ☎ *02/774-3890. www.mdsd.or.kr. Daily 9am–9pm. No masses and parish office closed Mon.*

❷ ★ ABC Mart. If you didn't pack comfortable shoes, this two-story shop is a perfect place to choose from thousands of name brands at affordable prices. There are also locations in Myeongdong and Gangnam. *52-5 Chungmuro 1(il)-ga, Jung-gu.* ☎ *02/771-7777. www.abcmart. co.kr. Daily 11am–11pm.*

❸ ★★ Myeongdong Gyoja. No one wants to shop on an empty stomach. So fill up on *mandu* (dumplings), *kal guksu* (hand-cut "knife" noodles) or *bibim guksu* (spicy mixed noodles) at this classic joint. The inexpensive food and unlimited refills of kimchi make it a popular dining spot for the area's hungry shoppers. Two locations in Myeongdong. *25-2 or 33-4 Myeongdong 2(i)-ga, Jung-gu.* ☎ *02/776-5348 or 02/776-3424. www.mdkj. co.kr. Daily 10:30am–9:30pm. $.*

Myeongdong Cathedral.

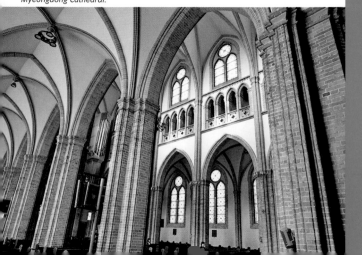

Shoppers at Myeongdong.

4 ★★ **Codes Combine.** Great trendy casual options for men, but plenty here for those of the fairer sex as well. Clothes are color-coded, making it easy to mix and match for the fashion-challenged. *53-11 Myeongdong 2(i)-ga, Jung-gu. 02/ 776-6385. www.codes-combine.com. Daily 10am–10pm.*

5 ★ **Migliore.** The name is synonymous with discount fashion, especially among the 20-something set. Its multiple floors are filled with small vendors selling clothing and accessories mostly for women, but there are options for men and children, too. *24-1 Chungmuro 1(il)-ga, Jung-gu. 02/2124-0001. www. migliore.co.kr. Tues–Sun 11am–11:30pm. Closed Mon. Connected to Myeongdong Station, line 4 (exit 5).*

6 **SPAO.** A Korean brand of comfortable, casual clothing for both genders, popular with some K-pop stars. They're known for their designer jeans and T-shirt collections. *24-23 Chungmuro 1(il)-ga, Jung-gu. 02/319-3850. www. spao.com. Mon–Thurs 11am–10pm, Fri–Sat until 10:30pm. Closed Sun.*

7 ★★★ **Ttrak of Bloo.** Perhaps Seoul's best record shop, and one of the few old-school shops in the area. Bypass the K-pop and make your way upstairs to the classical stacks or even farther up to the dusty vinyl on the third and fourth floors. *25-35 Chungmuro 1(il)-ga, Jung-gu. 02/778-7309.*

8 ★ **Shinsegae Department Store.** Korea's first department store (built in 1930), its multiple stories were renovated in 2005. Clothing for the whole family dominates the 1st through 8th floors, while the 9th floor is dedicated to home goods. If you're feeling a bit peckish, check out the food court and grocery in the basement. *52-50 Chungmuro 1(il)-ga, Jung-gu. 02/1588-1234. www.shinsegae. com/english. Daily 10:30am–8pm. Closed 1 rotating Mon a month.*

9 **Bank of Korea Museum.** The site of the first national bank is a neo-Renaissance building built in 1907. The museum has displays on the history of Korean currency and a good explanation of the country's banking system and monetary policy. You can also see your face on a South Korean bank note. ⏱ *30 min. 110 Namdaemunno 3(sam)-ga, Jung-gu. 02/759-4881. http://museum. bok.or.kr. Admission free. English audio guide available for ₩1,000. Tues–Sun 10am–5pm.*

⑩ ★★★ Wongudan Altar. Built in 1897 after the Chinese Temple of Heaven in Beijing. King Gojong had it built after declaring himself the "Son of Heaven" to perform the rite of heaven (a ritual of prayers offered to Heaven by the ruling king to ensure bountiful harvests). It was abolished in 1910 by the Japanese colonial government. Now it remains hidden on the grounds of the Westin Chosun as the last remnant of the short-lived Daehan Empire. 🕐 *30 min. 25-35 Chungmuro 1(il)-ga, Jung-gu (inside the grounds of the Westin Chosun).* ☎ *02/778-7309. Daily 24 hr.*

⑪ ★ Lotte Department Store. One of the most popular in the country, its flagship store opened here in Myeongdong in 1979. A food court and event hall are located in the basement, and sit-down restaurants can be found on the 11th and 12th floors. A duty-free shop is on the 10th floor with clothing, housewares, and luxury brands in between. Continue out into the Myeongdong Underground Shopping Center on your way to Euljiro 3(sam)-ga Station, if you haven't

Shinsaegae Department Store.

dropped from all the shopping. *Sogong-dong, Jung-gu.* ☎ *02/771-2500. www.lotteshopping.com. Daily 10:30am–8pm. Closed 1 rotating Mon a month.*

Seoul's Transportation

Seoul's subway system is an efficient web of public transport. The entire system is designed for ease of use by English-speakers, and all announcements and stations are clearly marked in English (a subway map is included in the back of this book). The bus system is efficient and far-reaching but more difficult to use, since none of the stops are written in English (though stops are announced in English on most buses). A pre-paid T-money (see the "Savvy Traveler" section) can be used on all forms of transport (including taxis that have the orange CARD cap on their roofs), as well as in certain convenience stores.

Seongbuk-dong

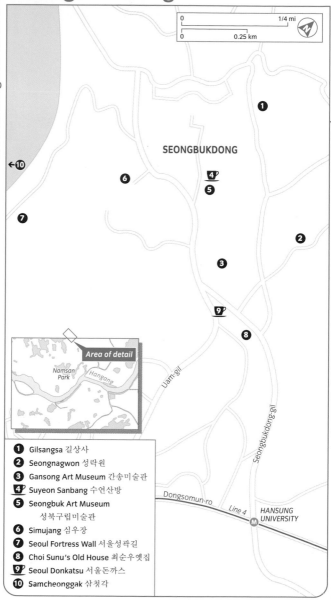

0   1/4 mi
0   0.25 km

SEONGBUKDONG

Area of detail

Namsan Park

Hangang

Uam-gil

Seongbukdong-gil

Dongsomun-ro   Line 4

HANSUNG UNIVERSITY

1 Gilsangsa 길상사
2 Seongnagwon 성락원
3 Gansong Art Museum 간송미술관
4 Suyeon Sanbang 수연산방
5 Seongbuk Art Museum
   성북구립미술관
6 Simujang 심우장
7 Seoul Fortress Wall 서울성곽길
8 Choi Sunu's Old House 최순우옛집
9 Seoul Donkatsu 서울돈까스
10 Samcheonggak 삼청각

They call Seongbuk-dong the "Beverly Hills" of Seoul, but that doesn't give justice to its stately, historic architecture. Nestled on the slopes of Bugaksan, it's home to not only some of the biggest mansions in the city, but also the homes of dozens of foreign ambassadors. The area is not well known to tourists but is worth a visit for its pretty gardens, unusual temple, and views, providing a quiet respite from the noisy city. It's a long uphill walk from the subway station, so it's best to take bus no. 1111 or 2112 to Sungbuk Elementary School, or the free shuttle to Gilsangsa (see below). **START: Hansung University Station, line 4 (exit 6).**

❶ ★★ Gilsangsa. Renovated in 1997, this temple has an unusual history. It was previously Daewon-gak, a former *yojeong*—an exclusive, private restaurant generally for male clientele to be served and entertained by young women, called *gisaeng*. It was donated by Kim Yeong-han, a former gisaeng and devout Buddhist, and has been a Zen center ever since. Overnight temple stays are offered the fourth weekend of each month. ⏱ *1 hr. 323-beonji Seongbuk 2(i)-dong, Seongbuk-gu.* ☎ *02/3672-5945. www.kilsangsa.or.kr (Korean only). Free shuttles in front of Dongwon Mart (just 30m past the bus no. 1111 stop) at 8:30am, 9:20am, 9:40am, 10am, noon, 1pm, 3pm and 4:30pm.*

❷ ★★★ Seongnagwon. A late-Joseon-era home of a high-ranking official under King Cheoljong (1849–1863). Later, the fifth son of King Gojong (Prince Yi Gang) spent his life here, dying in the home in 1955. Its grounds are one of the prime examples of Korean gardening, designed to harmonize the man-made with the natural, and is at its best in the spring or fall. ⏱ *45 min. 2-22 Seongbuk-dong, Seongbuk-gu.* ☎ *02/920-3410. Closed Sun.*

❸ ★ Gansong Art Museum. Korea's first private museum began as a collection by Jeon Hyeong-pil, who was saving national treasures from the Japanese colonialists.

Unfortunately, the collection is only viewable for 2 weeks in May and October, but the gardens are always open. ⏱ *30 min. 97-1 Seongbuk-dong, Seongbuk-gu.* ☎ *02/762-0442. Free admission.*

❹ ★★ Suyeon Sanbang. The smell of dried dates and cinnamon greet you as you enter this converted former home of novelist Yi Tae-jun, famous for being one of the fathers of modern Korean literature. His granddaughter serves traditional teas and rice cakes, but you'll be paying a bit extra for the atmosphere. *248 Seongbuk-dong, Seonbuk-gu.* ☎ *02/764-1736. $.*

Gilsangsa.

Seongnagwon.

5 Seongbuk Art Museum.
Located on the 2nd and 3rd floors of the Seongbuk Multicultural Village Center, this museum has rotating exhibits of contemporary artists. ⏱ *1 hr. 246 Seongbuk-dong,*

Suyeon Sanbang.

Seongbuk-gu. ☎ *02/920-3462. Closed Mon.*

6 ★ Shimujang. A Korean independence hero, Manhae Han Yong-un (1879–1944) lived here after his release, having been imprisoned for the March 1 independence movement. Unfortunately, he died here just before Korea's liberation in 1945. The name means "the place to find one's nature." ⏱ *30 min. 222-1-2 Seongbuk-dong, Seongbuk-gu. Free admission. Daily 24 hr.*

7 ★ Seoul Fortress Wall. The fortress wall was built around the old city during the Joseon Dynasty (1392–1910) over Bugaksan, Naksansa, Namsan, and Inwang. Originally 11 miles (18km) long, parts of it were destroyed in 1899; now only 10.5km of it remain. A walk along this small section of wall affords a nice view and a sense of history. ⏱ *1½ hr.*

8 ★★ Choi Sunu's Old House. Choi Sunu was the former president of the National Museum of Korea and a famous author. He lived in this hanok from 1976 until his death in 1984. It's been well preserved since

Samcheonggak.

it was designated a national monument. Guided tours are available by reservation. 🕐 *45 min. 126-20 Seongbuk 2(i)-dong, Seongbuk-gu. ☎ 02/3675-3401. http://nt-heritage.org/choisunu (Korean only). Closed Sun and Mon.*

9 Seoul Donkatsu. I don't know why, but this neighborhood has been known for its pork *bulgogi* (sliced rib-eye) and *donkatsu* (fried pork cutlet) joints since the 1980s. And this location will do you fine with juicy pork fried inside a crispy breaded outside and plenty of sauce to dip in. *131-85 Seonbuk-dong, Seongbuk-gu. ☎ 02/766-9370. $.*

10 ★★ Samcheonggak. The historic location of the joint talks in 2007 between North and South Korean representatives, it also used to be a famous salon for gisaeng. The Sejong Center for the Arts has managed it since 2009 and offers a variety of traditional cultural experiences for visitors. The lunch concerts include a set menu and a traditional tea for ₩50,000. Check the schedule for lunch concerts, traditional tea ceremonies, *hanbok* (traditional Korean costume) experiences, and other performances. *Time varies. 330-115 Seongbuk 2(i)-dong, Seongbuk-gu. ☎ 02/765-3700. Prices vary. Free shuttles available 10am–9:40pm from Gwanghwamun Station (exit 3) and City Hall Station (exit4), and in front of the Hyundai Gallery in Samcheongdong-gil.*

Hongdae-ap

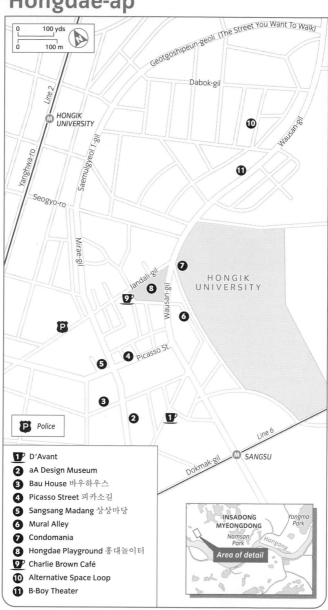

0 | 100 yds
0 | 100 m

Geotgoshipeun-geoli (The Street You Want To Walk)

Dabok-gil

Line 2

Yanghwa-ro

Ⓜ HONGIK UNIVERSITY

Seogyo-ro

Saemulgyeol 1-gil

Mirae-gil

Jandali-gil

Wausan-gil

Wausan-gil

Picasso St.

Ⓟ

HONGIK UNIVERSITY

Ⓟ Police

Line 6

Dokmak-gil

Ⓜ SANGSU

1🍵 D'Avant
2 aA Design Museum
3 Bau House 바우하우스
4 Picasso Street 피카소길
5 Sangsang Madang 상상마당
6 Mural Alley
7 Condomania
8 Hongdae Playground 홍대놀이터
9🍵 Charlie Brown Café
10 Alternative Space Loop
11 B-Boy Theater

INSADONG MYEONGDONG

Yongma Park

Namsan Park

Hangang

Area of detail

Hongik University ("Hongdae") is the country's foremost arts and design college. So it's no surprise that the area in front ("Hongdae-ap") is the center of Korea's indie culture. On weekends the streets are packed with people bar- or club-hopping, but there's more to Hongdae than its nightlife. It's a hotbed for young music, performance, art, and design—not to mention the many fun cafes and galleries in the area. See chapter 7 for Hongdae Club Day and other nightlife options. START: **Sangsu Station, line 6 (exit 2).**

1 ⭐⭐⭐ **D'Avant.** The place that started the Belgian waffle craze in Seoul, it's a favorite brunch spot for design lovers. Perfect for a leisurely brunch before hitting the town. *411-16 Seogyo-dong, Mapo-gu.* ☎ *02/325-5510. Daily 11am–11pm. $$.*

2 ⭐⭐ **aA Design Museum.** A multilevel gallery with a bit of an identity crisis. Design museum, shop, or cafe? Each floor has its own concept, but the whole joint is a win for vintage furniture fans. 🕐 *1 hr. 408-11 Seogyo-dong, Mapo-gu.* ☎ *02/3143-7311. www.aadesign museum.com.*

3 ⭐ **Bau House.** A boarding hotel and dog cafe, this is a place for canine lovers to bring their own best friend or just make a new one over a dog biscuit or two. (If you'd prefer some feline love, head to nearby Café Gio Cat at 3F, 358-92 Seogyo-dong). 🕐 *30 min. 405-13 Seogyo-dong, Mapo-gu.* ☎ *02/334-5152.*

4 **Picasso Street.** Named for all the galleries and artists that hang out in the area, it's fun just to browse the cafes and shops up and down the street. 🕐 *30 min.*

5 ⭐⭐⭐ **Sangsang Madang.** This 11-story art and design center has a great shop on the ground floor, galleries in between, and a cozy (but smoky) cafe on the sixth floor. There's a performance hall and movie theater in the basement levels. 🕐 *30 min. 367-5 Seogyo-dong, Mapo-gu.* ☎ *02/330-6200. Closed Mon.*

Mural Alley.

Hongik University.

6 ★ **Mural Alley.** Although it may be a little against the unwritten graffiti code, this outdoor gallery of sorts features changeable work from spray-paint artists. When facing the entrance to Hongik University, Mural Alley is to the right (see the map on p 50). ⏱ *15 min.*

7 ★ **Condomania.** In a country where sex is hush-hush and repressed, it's refreshing to see a colorful store celebrating the love glove. *360-5 Seogyo-dong, Mapo-gu.* ☎ *02/337-9139.*

Hongdae Free Market.

8 **Hongdae Playground.** If you're visiting on a Saturday or Sunday, be sure to catch the Free Market (p 65) or the Hope Market (p 66). During weekdays kids just play on the swings, but some nights the playground becomes a stage for impromptu punk bands.

9 ★ **Charlie Brown Café.** Decorated with Charles Schulz's creations, this modern cafe is a nice place to get a quiet coffee and dessert—that is, if you're not averse to eating Snoopy. *364-2 Seogyo-dong, Mapo-gu.* ☎ *02/332-2600. www.charliebrowncafe.net. $.*

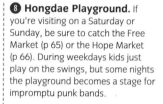

10 ★★ **Alternative Space Loop.** The first art space in Korea devoted to contemporary new art is still a showcase for emerging artists and experimental visionaries. ⏱ *30 min. 335-11 Seogyo-dong, Mapo-gu.* ☎ *02/3141-1377. http://galleryloop.com.*

11 **B-Boy Theater.** The rejuvenated break-dance culture is most apparent at this basement theater in the Samjin Pharmaceutical building. Performances most evenings, except Mondays. *338-8 Seogyo-dong, Mapo-gu.* ☎ *02/323-5233.* ●

Shopping Best Bets

Best **Second-Hand Shop**
★★★ Beautiful Store, *45 Anguk-dong, Jongno-gu (p 70)*

Best **Place for Electronics**
★★★ Yongsan Electronics Market, *Yongsan-gu (p 63)*

Best **Bookstore**
★★★ Kyobo Mungo, *1 Jongno 1(il)-ga, Jongno-gu (p 61)*

Best **Vintage Accessories**
★★ Bell & Nouveau, *540 Sinsa-dong, Gangnam-gu (p 70)*

Best **Shopping Mall**
★★ COEX Mall, *159 Samseong-dong, Gangnam-gu (p 68)*

Best **Department Store**
★★ Galleria, *515 Apgujeong-dong, Gangnam-gu (p 62)*

Best **Shoe Selection**
★★★ Designer Shoe Alley, *Cheongdam-dong, Gangnam-gu (p 68)*

Best **Hats**
★★★ Mogool, *545-10 Sinsa-dong, Gangnam-gu (p 65)*

Best **Tailor**
★★ Savile Row, *34-18 Itaewon-dong, Yongsan-gu (p 62)*

Best **Traditional Market**
★★★ Namdaemun Shijang, *Jongno-gu (p 70)*

Best **Women's Fashion Bargains**
★★★ Dongdaemun Shijang, *Dongdaemun (p 69)*

Best **Fabric Selection**
★★ Gwangjang Shijang, *Jongno-gu (p 63)*

Best **Antiques**
★★★ Dapsimni Antique Market, *Dapsimni (p 60)*

Best **Design Shop**
★★ Ssamzie Shop, *5-129 Changjeon-dong, Mapo-gu (Hongdae) (p 62)*

Best **Men's Fashions**
★★★ Volkswagen, *345-1 Seogyo-dong, Mapo-gu (p 65)*

Best **Record Shop**
★★★ Ttrak of Bloo, *25-35 Chungmuro 1(il)-ga, Jung-gu (p 44)*

Best **Unique Boutique**
★★★ Atelier & Project, *68-5 Seongbuk-dong, Seongbuk-gu (p 61)*

Shopping in Myeongdong.

Itaewon Shopping

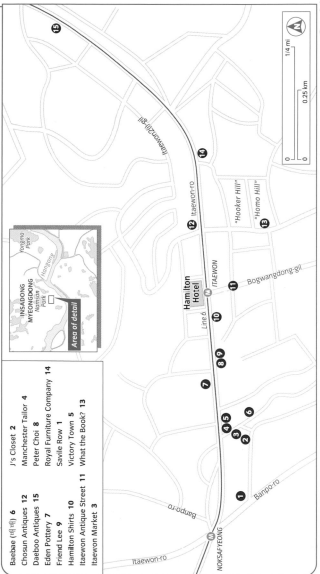

Photo p 530: Boutique in Sinsa-dong.

Seoul Shopping **Best Bets**

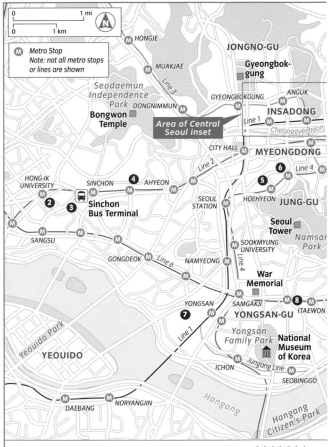

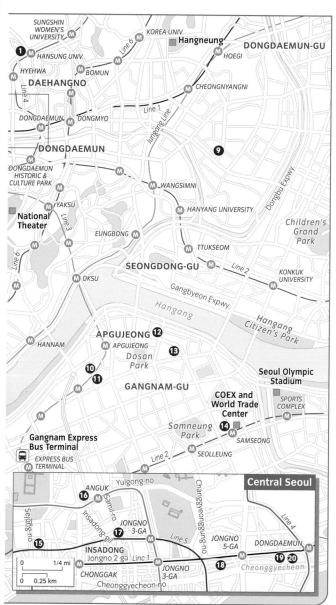

Garosu-gil Shopping

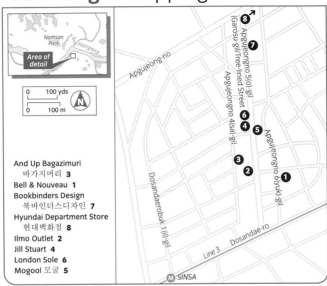

And Up Bagazimuri
바가지머리 **3**
Bell & Nouveau **1**
Bookbinders Design
북바인더스디자인 **7**
Hyundai Department Store
현대백화점 **8**
Ilmo Outlet **2**
Jill Stuart **4**
London Sole **6**
Mogool 모굴 **5**

Dongdaemun Shopping

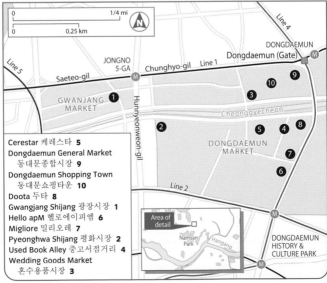

Cerestar 케레스타 **5**
Dongdaemun General Market
동대문종합시장 **9**
Dongdaemun Shopping Town
동대문쇼핑타운 **10**
Doota 두타 **8**
Gwangjang Shijang 광장시장 **1**
Hello apM 헬로에이피엠 **6**
Migliore 밀리오레 **7**
Pyeonghwa Shijang 평화시장 **2**
Used Book Alley 중고서점거리 **4**
Wedding Goods Market
혼수용품시장 **3**

Namdaemun Shopping

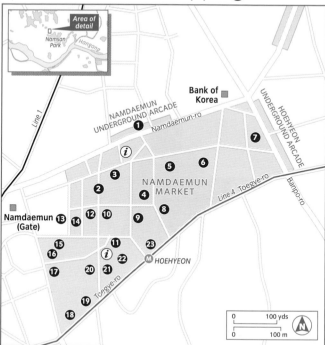

1. Namdaemun Underground Arcade
   남대문 수입상가
2. Namdaemun Food Street 남대문 먹자골목
3. Jung-ang Arcade/C-Dong imported goods, fashion, housewares C동중앙상가
4. Daedo Market women and children's clothes 대도마켓
5. Samik Shopping Town women's & kid's clothes, housewares 삼익쇼핑타운
6. Mesa men's, women's & kid's clothes
7. Shinsegae Department Store 신세계백화점
8. Common Plaza women's fashions 커먼프라자
9. Daedo Arcade Mall women's fashions 대도아케어드상점가
10. Daedo Jonghap Arcade/D-Dong housewares D동내도종합상가
11. Daedo Jonghap Arcade/E-Dongmen's, children's, housewares E동대도종합상가
12. Bondong Arcade food and agricultural products 본동상가
13. Sungnyemun Imported Goods Mall 숭례문수입상가
14. Namdaemun Arcade clothes & housewares 남대문상가
15. Namdo Jonghap Arcade imported goods & accessories 남대문종합상가
16. Yuseong Arcade accessories 유성상가
17. Jang-an Accessories Mall 장안악세서리상가
18. Yeonse Accessories Arcade 연세악세서리상가
19. Yeongchang Accessories Mall 연창악세서리상가
20. Gukje Imported Goods Mall 국제수입상가
21. Namdaemun No.1 Street women's fashions 남대문일가
22. Kennedy Arcade/Hanyoung Arcade 케네디/한영상가
23. Daedo women's fashions 대도

Shopping A to Z

Antiques

★★★ Dapsimni Antique Market
DAPSIMNI   The three buildings of this antiques market are filled with dozens of shops selling everything from tiny trinkets to wooden furniture from Korea's history. Prices range from ₩5,000 to more than ₩50 million. ☎ 02/2246-9122. Hours vary, but most Mon–Sat 10am–7pm. Subway: Dapsimni, line 5 (exit 2). Map p 56.

Kodosa INSADONG
The friendly owners will be happy to show you their collection of furniture, stone Buddha statues, and smaller pieces. 192-46 Gwanhun-dong, Jongno-gu. www.kodosa.co.kr. ☎ 02/735-5815.

Dapsimni Antique Market.

★ Gonghwarang INSADONG
Owned by the president of the Korean Antique Association, this shop specializes in old paintings and calligraphic works authenticated by the owner. 23-2 Insadong, Jongno-gu. ☎ 02/735-9938. Daily 10am–6:30pm.

Itaewon Antique Street
ITAEWON   It's no surprise that antiques shops hawking American and European wares can be found in the foreigner's district. Itaewon-dong, Yongsan-gu. Hours vary. Subway: Itaewon, line 6 (exit 3 or 4). Map p 55.

Jang-anpyeong Antique Market
DAPSIMNI   Vendors sell antiques and reproductions of traditional-style, everyday goods like eyeglasses, fish-shaped locks, silver knives, and ceramics at affordable prices. Also, several good furniture specialists are located at this market. Dongdaemun-dong, Dapsimni-gu.

☎ 02/797-8637. Hours vary. Subway: Gwangmyeongdang, line 5 (exit 2).

Beauty & Cosmetics

★ Etude House
MYEONGDONG   This Korean chain can be found all over the city, with five locations in Myeongdong alone. Its main store has the usual beauty products, a dollhouse gallery on the 2nd floor, and an art gallery on the 3rd. 31-7 Myeongdong 2(i)-ga, Jung-gu. ☎ 02/753-3771. www.etude.co.kr (Korean only). Daily 9 am–11 pm. Subway: Myeongdong, line 4 (exit 6).

The Face Shop
MYEONGDONG
With three locations in Myeongdong, this Korean brand offers beauty products for men, women, and even babies. 89-1 Euljiro 1(il)-ga, Jung-gu. ☎ 02/318-6577. www.thefaceshop.com. Daily 9:30am–10:30 pm. Subway: Euljiro 1(il)-ga, line 2 (exit 6).

Itaewon Antique Street.

Custom Made to Order

If you have the time and the inclination, Seoul is a wonderful city to get custom-fitted clothes. Itaewon is a popular area for foreigners to get suits and shirts tailor-made. Although there may be some argument about who provides the best workmanship, the little-known secret is that the tailors here send their orders to the same factory to be sewn, so there's very little variation in quality. Your best bet is to bring something that you like already and have them copy the styles and details for you. Most custom-made clothes take about a week; leather goods take about 2 weeks.

Books

★ Bandi & Lunis GANGNAM Its COEX Mall location has an extensive English-language book selection. Another location is in the basement of the Jongno Tower (subway: Jonggak, line 1, exit 2). *159 Samseong-dong, Gangnam-gu.* ☎ *02/1577-4030. www.bandinlunis.com. Daily 10:30am–10pm. Subway: Samseong, line 2 (exit 6).*

★★★ Kyobo Mungo JONGNO In the basement of its namesake building and in the Kyobo Gangnam Tower (subway: Gangnam, line 2, exit 6), it has a large selection of books, CDs, and DVDs, along with a cute stationery section. *1 Jongno 1(il)-ga, Jongno-gu.* ☎ *02/1544-1900. www.kyobobook.co.kr (Korean only). Daily 9:30am–10pm. Subway: Gwanghwamun, line 5 (exit 3). Map p 56.*

Royal Asiatic Society JONGNO Here you'll find a solid selection of books and some magazines in English about Korea. It also organizes lectures and tours of Korea. *Room 611, Korean Christian Bldg., Jongno-gu.* ☎ *02/763-9483. www.raskb. com. Mon–Fri 10am–noon and 2–5pm. Subway: Jongno 5(oh)-ga, line 1 (exit 2).*

★★ Seoul Selection JONGNO Inside the Korean Publishers Association building, this shop has a wide selection of books on Korean culture, CDs, and drama DVDs. *105-2 (B1), Sagan-dong, Jongno-gu.* ☎ *02/734-9565. www.seoul selection.com. Mon–Sat 9:30am–6:30pm. Subway: Anguk, line 3 (exit 1) or Ganghwamun, line 5 (exit 2).*

★★ What the Book ITAEWON It has a huge selection of used and new English titles and, if it doesn't have what you're looking for, can order it for you. The store will also deliver for free if you order more than three titles. *2F, 176-2 Itaewon-dong, Yongsan-gu.* ☎ *02/797-2342. www.whatthebook.com. Daily 10am–9pm. Subway: Itaewon, line 6 (exit 1). Map p 55.*

Boutique
★★★ Atelier & Project SEONG-BUK-DONG A unique shop started by three childhood friends, who grew up to be an art director, fashion curator, and pastry chef. They sell clothes, accessories, furniture, and flowers, and have a cafe. They also host art exhibits, cooking classes, and jazz concerts. *68-5 Seongbuk-dong, Seongbuk-gu.*

☎ 02/548-3374. www.atelierand project.com. Daily 11am–10pm. Subway: Hansung Univ., line 4 (exit 6). Map p 56.

★★ Ssamzie Shop HONGDAE-AP This multistoried arts complex has a cutting-edge design shop on the first floor filled with unique items from Korean and international industrial designers. The complex also houses contemporary art galleries, a theatre, a cafe, and studio spaces for young artists. 5-129 Changjeon-dong, Mapo-gu. ☎ 02/ 3142-1695. Subway: Sinchon, line 2 (exit 8).

Ceramics
★ Eden Pottery TAEWON Whether you're shopping for a celadon vase or an earthenware teacup, this cozy shop is a good place to look. 168-17 Itaewon-dong, Yongsan-gu. ☎ 02/793-0828. Daily 9am–7pm. Map p 55.

Custom Tailors
Hamilton Shirts ITAEWON It's been making custom men's dress shirts since 1976, right across the street from the Hamilton Hotel

Custom tailor in Itaewon.

(hence the name). A reasonable ₩30,000 to ₩40,000 per shirt. 736-9 Hannam-dong, Yongsan-gu. ☎ 02/798-5693. www.hs76.com. Map p 55.

★ Manchester Tailor ITAEWON Located in the basement level of the Gukje (Imported Goods) Arcade, this tailor has been fitting suits on men since 1969. 58-5 Itaewon-dong, Yongsan-gu. ☎ 02/790-7112. www. manchestertailor.net. Map p 55.

★★ Savile Row ITAEWON Although pricier than the competition, you'll always get high craftsmanship at this tailor. 34-18 Itaewon-dong, Yongsan-gu. ☎ 02/794-0887. Map p 55 and 56.

Department Stores
★★ Galleria APGUJEONG Known as the place for fashion, this store is unsurprisingly near Rodeo Street. Trendsetters shop here to get the top designer fashions before everyone else. Another location in Seoul Station. 515 Apgujeong-dong, Gangnam-gu. ☎ 02/3449-4114. www. galleria.co.kr (Korean only). Daily 10:30am–8pm. Subway: Apgujeong, line 3 (exit 1).

★ Hyundai APGUJEONG Since opening in 1985, this store has been setting trends across the country. If you want to see where Seoul's fashions will be heading, check out the clothes and accessories here. 429 Apgujeong-dong, Gangnam-gu. ☎ 02/547-2233. Daily 10:30am–8pm. Closed 1 variable Mon per month. Subway: Apgujeong, line 3 (exit 6). Map p 58 (top).

Lotte MYEONGDONG Since its first store in the late 1970s, Lotte has exploded. It now has six huge stores in Seoul, but this is their flagship. Sogong-dong, Jung-gu. ☎ 02/771-2500. www.lotteshopping. com. Daily 10:30am–8pm. Closed 1

Galleria department store.

variable Mon per month. Subway: Euljiro 1(il)-ga, line 2 (exit 2). Map p 42.

★ **Shinsegae** NAMDAEMUN The oldest department store in the country, it started out as a Japanese store during the Japanese occupation in the 1930s and was given its current name in 1963. Although it has other locations, this is the original. Renovated in 2008, it has 14 stories of shopping and eating fun. *52-5 Chungmuro 1(il)-ga, Jung-gu.* ☎ *02/1588-1234. Daily 10:30am–8pm. Subway: Hoehyeon, line 4 (exit 7). Map p 59.*

Electronics
★★★ **Yongsan Electronics Market** YONGSAN A grouping of 22 buildings and thousands of small shops, it has every electronic gadget, part, or equipment imaginable. The largest collections are in the Terminal Electronics Market, Seonin, and I'Park Mall, each specializing in specific products. Najin Market is the most crowded but has the best bargains. Most eateries in the area are geared toward the vendors, but you'll find good options on levels 4, 5, and 6 of I'Park Mall. *15-2 Hangan-gro 2(i)-ga, Yongsan-gu.* ☎ *02/704-3060. Most shops daily 10am–8pm. Closed 1st and 3rd Sun of every*

month. Flea market every weekend 9am–7pm. www.yongsan.co.kr (Korean only). Subway: Yongsan, line 1 (exit 2) or Sin-Yongsan, line 4 (exit 5). Map p 56.

Fabric
★★★ **Dongdaemun Shopping Town** DONGDAEMUN Located across Cheonggyecheon from Pyeonghwa Shijang, the four floors of fabric (silk, wools, cotton, fake fur, and more) are a dream for the crafty. The fifth floor has beads and findings for jewelry makers. The basement is full of lace, sequin, buttons, and other sewing notions. Look for the large white building. *Euljiro 6(yook)-ga, Jung-gu.* ☎ *02/2262-0114. www. dongdaemunsc.co.kr (mostly Korean). Subway: Dongdaemun, line 1 or 4 (exit 9). Map p 58 (bottom).*

★★ **Gwangjang Shijang** JONGNO Since 1905, it's been a great place to get textiles, silks, blankets, and more. The second floor has bedsheets, satin, and quilts. You can also get custom-made *hanbok* (Korean traditional outfits). See p 32 for food info. *6-1 Yeji-dong, Jongno-gu.* ☎ *02/2267-0291. Daily 7am–7pm. Closed some Tues. Subway: Jongno 5(oh)-ga, line 1 (exit 8). Map p 58 (bottom).*

Department Stores

Towering, multilevel department stores can be found in every neighborhood in Seoul. They have similar layouts, with the basement floor full of groceries and inexpensive food courts. Brand-name cosmetics and jewelry are on the first floor. The middle floors display clothing, with higher floors selling furniture, home goods, and sports supplies. The top floor (or two) is usually loaded with more expensive restaurants. *Tip:* For 2 weeks each season, the stores have sales (usually in Jan, Apr, July, and Oct).

Fashion

And Up Bagazimuri SINSA-DONG This tiny boutique shop has unique women's clothes and accessories with new stock coming in daily. *535-4 Sinsa-dong, Gangnam-gu. ☎ 02/541-8241. www.bagazimuri. com (Korean only). Subway: Sinsa, line 3 (exit 8). Map p 58 (top).*

★ **Ann Demeulemeester** GANG-NAM The Belgian designer's latest shop is housed in a fascinating building, covered with living green plants. You can't miss the soft

Fabric at Dongdaemun Shopping Town.

green, rectangular building with undulating glass windows and staircases. There's a rooftop restaurant and basement multi-shop. *650-14 Sinsa-dong, Gangnam-gu. ☎ 02/3442-2570. www.anndemeulemeester.be. Subway: Gangnam-gu Office, line 7 (exit 3 or 4).*

Jill Stuart SINSA-DONG Spanning two floors of women's fashions, its pink and white exterior belies what's inside. *535-14 Sinsa-dong, Gangnam-gu. ☎ 02/541-0636. www.jillstuart. com. Daily noon–9pm. Subway: Sinsa, line 3 (exit 8). Map p 58 (top).*

★★ **Kosney** MYEONGDONG Although it brands itself a "lifestyle" shop, the cute home goods are overshadowed by the clothing selection. *B1, 32-11 Myeongdong 2(i)-ga, Jung-gu. ☎ 02/778-5009. www.kosney.co.kr. Subway: Myeongdong, line 4 (exit 6).*

Lotte Young Plaza MYEONG-DONG Since 2003, it has been the go-to location to find for fashion-able casual wear for the 20-some-thing set. *1-beonji, Sogong-dong, Jung-gu. ☎ 02/771-2500. Daily 11:30am–9:30pm. Closed 1 rotating Mon per month. Subway: Euljiro, line 2 (exit 6).*

★ **Migliore** DONGDAEMUN Several floors of clothes and accessories for the whole family, but most of the floors are geared toward women in their 20s. There's also one in Myeongdong. *18-145 Euljiro 6(yook)-ga, Jung-gu. ☎ 02/3393-0001. www.migliore.co.kr (Korean only). Tues–Sun 10:30am–5pm. Map p 58 (bottom).*

★★ 10 Corso Como CHEONG-DAM-DONG   A favorite among Korean celebrities, this store has not only designer fashions, but a wine bar, bookstore, and music shop, too. *79 Cheongdam-dong, Gangnam-gu. ☎ 02/3018-1010. www.10corsocomo.co.kr. Daily 11am–8pm (cafe keeps longer hours). Subway: Apgujeong, line 3 (exit 1).*

Victory Town ITAEWON   A marketplace selling mostly designer overruns and knock-offs, head up to the third floor for larger sizes. *58 Itaewon-dong, Yongsan-gu. ☎ 02/798-4040. Daily 9am–7pm. Subway: Itaewon, line 6 (exit 4). Map p 55.*

Fashion—Accessories

★ Baebae ITAEWON   The owner designs the hip shoes and jewelry at this accessory shop popular with Korean celebs. Skull rings and pop themes abound. *59-3 Itaewon-dong, Yongsan-gu. ☎ 02/790-5180. www.baebae.net. Subway: Itaewon, line 6 (exit 4). Map p 55.*

★★★ Mogool SINSA-DONG   Trucker hats, berets, casquettes, bowlers, and more—they've got every style and color to fit your head on Apgujeong's Garosu-gil. *545-10 Sinsa-dong, Gangnam-gu. ☎ 02/3445-6211. www.mogool.co.kr. Subway: Sinsa, line 3 (exit 8). Map p 56 and 58 (top).*

Fashion—Bridal

★★ Ahyeon-dong Wedding Street IDAE-AP   Sinchonno Road is lined with dozens of wedding-dress shops. Although most of them specialize in custom, white wedding gowns, some shops also customize hanbok. Just give them a week to put it all together for you. *Bukahyeon-dong, Seodaemun-gu. Most shops daily 10am–10 pm. Subway: Ewha Womans Univ., line 2 (exit 4 or 5).*

Fashion—Men's

★★ Volkswagen HONGDAE-AP   One of the few men's shops in the area, it carries T-shirts, jeans, hats, and man-bags. *345-1 Seogyo-dong, Mapo-gu. ☎ 02/334-8817. Subway: Hongik Univ., line 2 (exit 5).*

Fashion—Outlet

A&H NY State Outlet SINSA-DONG   New items come every week from American department stores and are sold here at deep discounts of 50% to 90%. Don't miss the basement floor. *545-5 Sinsa-dong, Gangnam-gu. ☎ 02/544-0229. www.aandh.co.kr. Daily 10:30am–9pm. Subway: Sinsa, line 3 (exit 8).*

Ilmo Outlet SINSA-DONG   Markdowns (up to 80%) of designer names can be found on the second floor. There's a cafe (Scoop Garden) and full-priced fashions on the first floor. *535-13 Sinsa-dong, Gangnam-gu. ☎ 02/515-0970. www.aandh.co.kr. Daily 11am–9pm. Subway: Sinsa, line 3 (exit 8). Map p 58 (top).*

Fashion—Korean Traditional

See **Gwangjang Shijang** (p 63) and **Dongdaemun Shijang** (p 69).

Flea Markets

★★ Hongdae Free Market HONGDAE-AP   From March to November, students set up shop at this open-air flea market at the playground in front of Hongik University. You'll find handmade crafts, dolls, clothes, accessories, and a variety

Bargaining Tips

Seoul's open-air markets are a bargain-hunter's paradise. Vendors sell everything from piles of clothes to costume jewelry from mobile carts and open storefronts. Be ready to barter your way to a better deal, especially if you're paying cash. Wholesale dealers in Dongdaemun and Namdaemun will give you a better deal if you buy in bulk; sellers in Itaewon expect you to haggle the price down. Don't worry about offending the storeowners; if the price you call is too low, they'll definitely let you know.

of knickknacks, since the unwritten rule is to sell nothing from factories. *www.freemarket.or.kr (Korean only). Sat 1–6pm (closed for rain/snow). Subway: Hongik Univ., line 2 (exit 6). Map p 50.*

★ Hongdae Hope Market

HONGDAE-AP   Also at the Hongdae playground, this open-air market happens on Sundays from March to November. Students and artists hawk handmade wares or draw portraits for just a few thousand won. *www.freemarket.or.kr. Sun 2–6pm (closed for rain/snow). Subway: Hongik Univ., line 2 (exit 6). Map p 50.*

Pungmul Shijang JONGNO

Seoul's historic *o-il shijang* (5-day flea market) has a permanent home in a two-story building (after moving when Cheonggyecheon was built) with plenty of sellers spilling out into the nearby streets. It has more than 900 vendors selling everything from folk objects to clothing, to food and souvenirs. *Jongno-gu. Daily 10am–7pm. Subway: Sinseoldong, line 1 or 2 (exit 9).*

Furniture

★ Chosun Antiques ITAEWON

Although the name says "antique," it also sells high-quality new furniture made in the traditional style. The store will even pack and deliver

or ship for you. *124-5 Itaewon 1(il)-dong, Yongsang-gu.* ☎ *02/793-3726. Subway: Itaewon, line 6 (exit 2). Map p 55.*

★ Daeboo Antiques ITAEWON

A veritable treasure-trove of antiques and more affordable reproductions await you, as well as the owner's friendly dog. *739-12 Hannam-dong, Yongsan-gu.* ☎ *02/797-6787. Daily 10am–6:30pm. Subway: Hangangjin, line 6 (exit 1). Map p 55.*

★★ Royal Furniture Company

ITAEWON   The kind older couple here can help you pick out a traditional Korean piece and make arrangements for shipping overseas. *137-2 Bogwang-dong, Yongsan-gu.* ☎ *02/797-8637. www.royal-antique.com. Daily 9am–7pm. Map p 55.*

Jewelry

★★ Jongno Jewelry District

JONGNO   Literally hundreds of wholesale jewelry shops are grouped together in this area between Jongno 1(il)-ga and Jongno 5(oh)-ga. The shops in the alley behind the Dansungsa Theater and those on the first floor of the Dansungsa building specialize in precious jewels and metals. Watches and wedding gift shops are located in the Yeji-dong alley in Jongno

4(sa)-ga. Be sure to get an A/S warranty card and a certificate of authenticity when you buy. *Jongno-gu. Daily 9am–9:30pm. Subway: Jongno 3(sam)-ga, line 1 or 3 (exit 10 or 11; exit 12 for the jewelry "department store").*

★★ Gangnam Precious Jewels and Metals Complex GANG-NAM

Although not as large as the Jongno complex, the stores here are easier to navigate since they're all located in one building. Most of them sell to the wholesale market, but some are willing to sell directly as well. *Reubon City, 1F, Banpo-dong, Seocho-gu. ☎ 02/591-4441. Tues–Sun 10am–8pm. Subway: Express Bus Terminal, line 3 or 7 (exit toward Honamseon) or exit 8, through Shinsegae Dept. Store, exit the main doors and go left toward Banpo Bridge.*

★ Lloyd GANGNAM

This jewelry shop, which specializes in mostly gold and silver pieces, is popular with younger shoppers. The main shop is located inside the COEX Mall. *C-23, COEX B1, 159 Samseong-dong, Gangnam-gu. ☎ 02/6002-6257. www.lloydgift.com. Daily 10:30am–10:30pm.*

Leather Goods

Friend Lee ITAEWON   All the items in the store can be fitted or altered to your size, and you can even get any leather pieces custom-made to your liking. *72-35 Itaewon-dong, Yongsan-gu. ☎ 02/796-8519. Daily 9am–7pm. Subway: Itaewon, line 6 (exit 4). Map p 55.*

★ J's Closet ITAEWON

Vintage wear sits next to custom-designed leather dresses and many one-of-a-kind finds. *56-10 Itaewon-dong, Yongsan-gu. ☎ 02/543-7333. www.jscloset.co.kr. Subway: Noksapyeong, line 6 (exit 3). Map p 55.*

Peter Choi ITAEWON   The shop sells high-quality leather jackets, handbags, wallets, and more. If you're wiling to wait 2 weeks, you can even get things custom-made. *72-35 Itaewon-dong, Yongsan-gu. ☎ 02/798-8734. Daily 9:30am–9pm. Subway: Itaewon, line 6 (exit 4). Map p 55.*

Musical Instruments

★★★ Nakwon Musical Instruments Arcade INSADONG

A giant mecca for musicians, dozens of shops here sell traditional instruments like *daegeum* (bamboo flutes), *gayageum* (Korean "zither"), imported guitars, and everything you need to start your band. *Insa-dong, Jongno-gu. ☎ 02/924-0604. Mon–Sat 10am–7:30pm. Subway: Jongno 3(sam)-ga, line 1 or 5 (exit 5).*

Shoes

★★ ABC Mart MYEONGDONG

See p 43. *52-5 Chungmuro 1(il)-ga, Jung-gu. ☎ 02/771-7777. www.abcmart.co.kr. Daily 10am–10pm. Subway: Myeongdong, line 4 (exit 6 or 8). Map p 42.*

Decorative sign on Apgujeong Rodeo Street.

★★★ Designer Shoe Alley

APGUJEONG   In a little alley behind the Gucci store on Rodeo Street are a hidden handful of Korean designer shoe stores, with unique styles that won't be copied for at least another year. Korean shoe sizes may be too small, but if you have the time, they can custom-order shoes for you within a week. *Cheongdam-dong, Gangnam-gu. Subway: Cheongdam, line 7; or Apgujeong, line 3.*

★★ London Sole

SINSA-DONG   Specializing in ballet flats and specialty designs, this international celebrity favorite has a boutique in Garosu-gil. You can't miss its baby-pink facade. *534-13 Sinsa-dong (Dongyeong Bldg. 101-ho), Gangnam-gu.* ☎ *02/549-3691. www.fashionbliss.co.kr (Korean only). Mon–Sat 10:30am–10pm. Map p 58 (top).*

★★ Sue Comma Bonnie

APGUJEONG   Although more than a handful of these shops are located around town (including in the Galleria and the Lotte department store), loyal followers swear the "designer shoe alley" location is the best. A fresh and youthful Korean brand, you'll pay for the exclusivity.

96-5 Cheongdam-dong, Gangnam-gu. ☎ *02/3443-0217. Daily 10am–10pm. Subway: Apgujeong, line 3 (exit 1 or 2).*

★ 10 Selection

SAMCHEONG-DONG   A boutique shoe store on the main street, it sells unique styles from Korean designers. *62-8 Samcheong-dong, Jongno-gu.* ☎ *02/733-6525. Tues–Sun 7am–5pm. Subway: Anguk, line 3 (exit 1).*

Shopping Centers & Malls

★★ COEX Mall

GANGNAM   A giant megamall, it's home to more than 250 stores and dozens of eating places. It also includes a movie theater (with 16 screens), a nightclub, banks, a post office, **Bandi & Lunis** (p 61), the COEX Aquarium, and the Kimchi Museum. *159 Samseong-dong, Gangnam-gu.* ☎ *02/6002-5312. www.coex.co.kr. Daily 10am–10pm. Subway: Samseong, line 2 (exit 5 or 6).*

Doota

DONGDAEMUN   Several stories of fashion start on the second basement floor and go up to the food court on the seventh floor, with shops open well into the early dawn hours. *18-12 Euljiro*

Sinsa-dong garosu-gil.

Doota.

6(yook)-ga, Jung-gu. ☎ 02/3398-3333. www.doota.com. Mon 7pm–5am (next day); Tues–Sat 10:30am–5am; Sun 10:30am–11pm. Subway: Dongdaemun, line 1 (exit 8) or line 4 (exit 5). Map p 58 (bottom).

Noon Square MYEONGDONG
This mirrored glass block is designed after a snow crystal (*noon* means "snow" in Korean). Inside you'll find international fashion brands, restaurants, a bookstore, and a CGV theater. *83-5 Myeongdong 2(i)-ga, Jung-gu. ☎ 02/3783-5005. www. noonsquare.co.kr. Daily 11am–10pm. Subway: Myeongdong, line 4 (exit 6).*

Stationery
Bookbinders Design SINSA-DONG Swedish-designed journals, photo albums, stamps, notebooks, and other paper goods are available in a rainbow of colors. *547-2 Sinsa-dong (Dongseong Bldg.), Gangnam-gu. ☎ 02/516-1155. www.book bindersdesign.co.kr (Korean only). Daily 11am–10pm. Subway: Sinsa, line 3 (exit 8). Map p 58 (top).*

Note: Kyobo Mungo also has a great stationery section.

Toys
Puzzle Zone GANGNAM Sure, it has a huge selection of jigsaw puzzles, but the real treasures are the miniature models (for sale) of old Korean palaces, houses, and boats. *COEX Mall O-17, 159 Samseong-dong, Gangnam-gu. ☎ 02/6002-3578.*

Traditional Markets
★★★ Dongdaemun Shijang
DONGDAEMUN Opened in 1905, this major shopping area is sprawling. Modern, multistoried fashion malls (like Doota and Migliore) rise up on one side, while the other side has the traditional open-air stalls. One section mainly sells clothing wholesale. There is an area for wedding goods, an alley of used book vendors, and more than 30,000 little shops, some open 24 hours. *Jongno-gu. ☎ 02/2254-3300. Subway: Dongdaemun History & Culture Park, line 2 or 4 (exit 2 or 3). Most shops daily 10am–5am. Map p 56.*

For **Gwangjang Shijang**, see p 63.

Dongdaemun Shijang.

★★★ Gyeongdong Shijang

JEGI   The country's most famous Oriental medicine marketplace has hundreds of shops selling roots, dried mushrooms, and everything for *hanyak* (herbal medicine). It's a fun place to see, smell, touch, and taste unusual things, like dried millipedes and unidentifiable barks. The traditional market that spills into it is crowded with middle-age ladies carting home vegetables for the week's dinners. *Jegi-dong, Dongdaemun-gu.* ☎ *02/967-8721. www. kyungdongmart.com (Korean only). Daily 9am–7pm. Closed 1st and 3rd Sun of every month. Subway: Jegi, line 1 (exit 2).*

Itaewon Market ITAEWON

The foreigners area makes shopping easy for English-speakers, but it also means prices are inflated to trap tourists, so be sure to bargain down. *Itaewon-dong, Yongsan-gu. Hours vary. Subway: Noksapyeong, line 6 (exit 3). Map p 55.*

A department store in Dongdaemun Shijang.

★★★ Namdaemun Shijang

JONGNO   The country's largest traditional market since the 1400s, Namdaemun (which means "great south gate") market is chock-full of shops and carts piled high with clothing, housewares, food, and accessories. Most shops sell directly from their own factories. Step into the tall buildings for more options and wholesale dealers. *49 Namchang-dong, Jung-gu. No set hours, but most shops daily 9am–9pm. Night market daily midnight–4am. Subway: Hoehyeon, line 4 (exit 5 or 6). Map p 56.*

Vintage Stores

★★★ Beautiful Store INSA-

DONG   A bargain hunter's paradise, clothes go for ₩3,000 and up. Upstairs it has CDs, art objects, books, and household items. Profits go to Asian Oxfam. There's another location in Hongdae-ap. *45 Angukdong, Jongno-gu.* ☎ *02/1577-1113. www.beautifulstore.org. Mon–Sat 10:30am–6pm. Subway: Anguk, line 3 (exit 4).*

★★ Bell & Nouveau SINSA-

DONG   Vintage jewelry, hats, glasses, and more, sold by friendly staff. *B1, 540 Sinsa-dong (Myoungho Bldg.), Gangnam-gu.* ☎ *02/517-5521. www.bellnouveau.com (mostly Korean). Daily 11am–10pm. Subway: Sinsa, line 3 (exit 8). Map p 56 and 58.*

Jou Joux HONGDAE-AP   A cute lit-

tle shop with vintage finds for the whole family, though most of the selections are geared toward women. *347-17 Seogyo-dong, Mapo-gu.* ☎ *02/333-3627. Also on the 2nd floor of Gwangjang Shijang (p 58 [bottom]). www.cyworld.com/joujoux (Korean only). Daily 11am–10pm. Subway: Sangsu, line 6 (exit 1) or Hongdae, line 2 (exit 8 or 9).* ●

Namsan

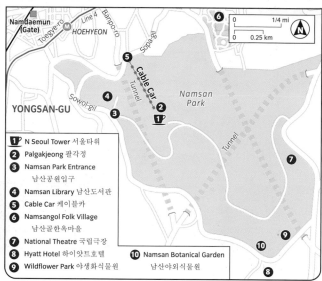

YONGSAN-GU

1. N Seoul Tower 서울타워
2. Palgakjeong 팔각정
3. Namsan Park Entrance
   남산공원입구
4. Namsan Library 남산도서관
5. Cable Car 케이블카
6. Namsangol Folk Village
   남산골한옥마을
7. National Theatre 국립극장
8. Hyatt Hotel 하이얏트호텔
9. Wildflower Park 야생화식물원
10. Namsan Botanical Garden
    남산야외식물원

Bukhansan National Park

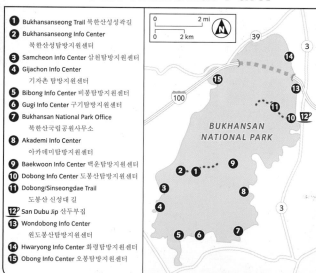

1. Bukhansanseong Trail 북한산성성곽길
2. Bukhansanseong Info Center
   북한산성탐방지원센터
3. Samcheon Info Center 삼천탐방지원센터
4. Gijachon Info Center
   기자촌 탐방지원센터
5. Bibong Info Center 비봉탐방지원센터
6. Gugi Info Center 구기탐방지원센터
7. Bukhansan National Park Office
   북한산국립공원사무소
8. Akademi Info Center
   아카데미탐방지원센터
9. Baekwoon Info Center 백운탐방지원센터
10. Dobong Info Center 도봉산탐방지원센터
11. Dobong/Sinseongdae Trail
    도봉산 신성대 길
12. San Dubu Jip 산두부집
13. Wondobong Info Center
    원도봉산탐방지원센터
14. Hwaryong Info Center 화령탐방지원센터
15. Obong Info Center 오봉탐방지원센터

Previous page: Bridge at Namsan Park.

Cheonggyecheon

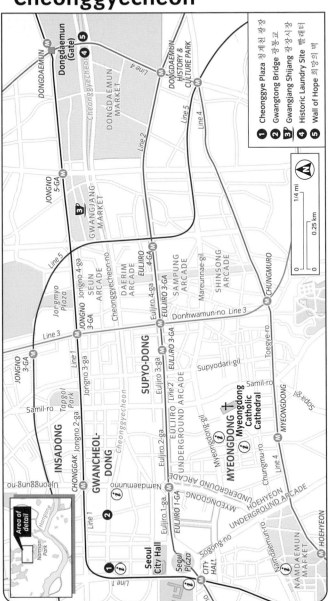

1/4 mi

0   0.25 km

Dongdaemun (Gate)

DONGDAEMUN

DONGDAEMUN HISTORY & CULTURE PARK

DONGDAEMUN MARKET

Line 4

Cheonggyecheon

JONGNO 5-GA

GWANGJANG MARKET

Line 5

Line 2

Line 5

Line 4

JONGNO 4-GA

Jongno 4-ga

SEUN ARCADE

DAERIM ARCADE

Cheonggyecheon-no

EULJIRO 4-GA

SAMPUNG ARCADE

SHINSONG ARCADE

Mareunnae-gil

Jongmyo Plaza

JONGNO 3-GA

EULJIRO 3-GA

Euljiro 4-ga

Donhwamun-no Line 3

CHUNGMURO

Line 5

Line 3

JONGNO 3-GA

Line 1

Jongno 3-ga

SUPYO-DONG

EULJIRO 3-GA

Euljiro 3-ga

Supyodari-gil

Samil-ro

INSADONG

Tapgol Park

CHONGGAK

Jongno 2-ga

Samil-ro

EULJIRO Line 2

EUL.RO 3-GA

Euljiro 2-ga

MYEONGDONG

Myeongdong Catholic Cathedral

Myeongdong-gil

MYEONGDONG

Sogong-gil

Ujeonggguk-no

GWANCHEOL-DONG

Cheonggyecheon

Namdaemunno

EULJIRO MYEONGDONG UNDERGROUND ARCADE

Chungmu-ro

Line 4

Toegye-ro

HOEHYEON

Line 1

Euljiro 1-ga

EULJIRO 1-GA

Euljiro 1-ga

MYEONGDONG UNDERGROUND ARCADE

HOEHYEON UNDERGROUND ARCADE

Namdaemun-ro

NAMDAEMUN MARKET

Seoul City Hall

Seoul Plaza

CITY HALL

Sogong-no

Line 1

Area of detail

Namsan Park

Hoegang

The Great Outdoors

Olympic Park

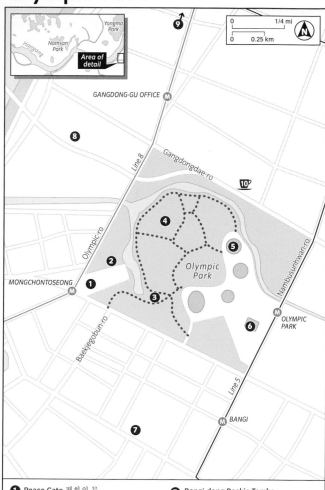

1 Peace Gate 평화의 문
2 Seoul Olympic Museum
   서울올림픽기념관
3 SOMA Museum 소마미술관
4 Mongchon Earthen Fortress 몽촌토성
5 Indoor Swimming Pool 실내수영장
6 Tennis Courts
   테니스장 or 테니스 코트
7 Bangi-dong Baekje Tombs
   방이동백제고분군
8 Pungnap Earthen Fortress 풍납토성
9 Amsa-dong Prehistoric Settlement Site
   암사동선사주거지
10 Soho 소호

Seoul Parks & **Outdoor Spaces**

Seoul is better known for its sprawling apartment complexes than for its green spaces. However, there are plenty of mountains and parks to explore. On weekends you'll see hoards of Koreans, young and old alike, with their visors and hiking gear making their way up steep inclines on Seoul's outskirts. We've compiled a few places where you can get away from the hustle and bustle of the crowded city.

Namsan

★★ **Namsan Park Trails.** Namsan is more of a large hill than a mountain, but it is conveniently located in the middle of the city. There are several trails that wind their way to the top and the **N Seoul Tower** (p 16), which affords a nice view on a clear day. Stop at the lower-level food court for lunch before heading back down. ☎ *02/3783-5900. Subway: Hoehyeon, line 4 (exit 4), Chungmuro, line 4 (exit 2), or Dongguk Univ., line 3 (line 6). Then, take bus no. 0014 to the National Theater, the Hyatt for the botanical garden, or the Namsan library for the park entrance and stairs. Bus no. 02 takes you almost to the top. Map p 72.*

Steps at Namsan Park.

Lunch Break

Stop at the P1 level food court of the N Seoul Tower for lunch before heading back down. There are plenty of Korean "fast food" options, like *gimbap* (seaweed rice rolls) and noodles. Or grab a drink and a light lunch at Coffee & Sandwich. *Yongsan-dong 2(i)-ga, Yongsan-gu.* ☎ *02/3455-9277. $.*

Namsan Botanical Garden. There are thousands of plants here, categorized by theme. Although the garden is open year-round, it's best viewed in the spring and fall. *Free admission. Mar–Oct Tues–Sun*

Namsan cable car.

9am–6pm; Nov–Feb Tues–Sun 9am–5pm. Bus: 402 or 0014. Map p 72.

Wildflower Park. Although the name implies a field of wild flowers, there are also trees, bamboo, fern, and other plants that grace this garden. *772-12 Hannam-dong, Yongsan-gu. Free admission. Open daily 24 hr. Bus: 402 or 0014. Map p 72.*

Cheonggyecheon

Cheonggye Plaza. The plaza is where this stream starts. The "cheon" runs 3⅔ miles (5¾km) through downtown Seoul. A natural stream, it was covered up to make a road in 1958. It was reopened as a stream again in 2005 and affords an ant's-eye view of the city on either side. *31 Taeyeong-no 1(il)-ga, Jung-gu. Subway: Jegi-dong, line 1 (exit 4), a 15-min. walk; or Yongdu, line 2 (exit 5), a 10-min. walk. Map p 73.*

Gwangtong-gyo. Of the 22 bridges that crossed Cheonggye stream, this was the largest. Originally built for Joseon Dynasty royalty, it was restored and moved about 164 yards (150m) upstream from its original location. *Subway: Jonggak, line 1; or Euljiro 1(il)-ga, line 2. Map p 73.*

Historic Laundry Site. Back in olden times, women used to come here to hand-wash their laundry. There's a small homage to them between Dasan and Yeongdo bridges. *Subway: Dongdaemun, line 4 (exits 7 or 8). Map p 73.*

Gwangjang Shijang

Climb up the stairs to Gwangjang market and stop for snack or lunch from one of the dozens of vendors cooking delicious Korean fare in the marketplace. *See p 63. Most vendors closed Sun. $.*

Cheonggyecheon.

World Peace Gate.

Wall of Hope. More than 20,000 ceramic tiles line walls on either side of Cheonggyecheon. Each one is handmade by both Korean and international artists hoping for reunification of the two Koreas. *Map p 73.*

Olympic Park

★★ Olympic Park. At the site of the Mongchon Earthen Fortress (from the early Baekje Period), the city built this massive park to host the 1988 Olympics. The **Seoul Olympic Museum** commemorates that event, and the **SOMA Museum of Art** holds rotating contemporary art exhibits. There also are more than 200 outdoor sculptures sent here from different countries as a gift to the host city. The park is a nice place for a leisurely walk, in-line skating, or a swim in the on-site pool. *Subway: Mongchontoseong, line 8 (exit 1) for the Peace Gate and museum; Olympic Park, line 5 (exit 3) for the gymnasiums and the pool. Map p 74.*

Grilled Beef at Soho

If you've worked up an appetite from all that walking, stop in for some grilled beef at nearby joint Soho. It has reasonable prices and the usual tabletop grills in a casual atmosphere. *460-2 Seongnae-dong, Gangdong-gu.* ☎ *02/471-9263. Daily 11am–11pm. $$.*

Bangi-dong Baekje Tombs. Only eight tombs remain from the early Baekje Period (A.D. 200–475), but they're pretty typical of stone chambers and the soil mounds from that time. ☎ *02/410-3661. Free*

Detail at Gwangtong bridge.

The Great **Outdoors**

In-line skating at Olympic Park.

peninsula. ☎ *02/410-3776. Subway: Cheonho, line 5; then take bus no. 3312. Map p 74.*

Amsa-dong Prehistoric Settlement Site. On the edge of the Han River, this prehistoric site was discovered during a flood in 1925. It's said to date back to Neolithic times, around 6000 B.C. ☎ *02/3426-3867. Tues–Sun 9:30am–6pm. Subway: Amsa, line 8 (exit 1). Map p 74.*

Bukhansan National Park

Bukhansan is located in the northern part of Seoul and stretches across to Yangju-gun in Gyeonggi-do. Not only will you get fabulous views of the city from its peaks, but the lovely granite formations make the visit worthwhile. Although dozens of trails zigzag through the mountain, we've outlined two solid hikes, both requiring a moderate level of fitness. The times given are for round-trip to the peaks and back.

★★★ **Bukhansanseong Trail.** One of the most popular trails in the

admission. Daily Mar–Oct 9am–6pm; Nov–Feb 9am–5pm. Subway: Bangi, line 5 (exit 3). Map p 74.

Pungnap Earthen Fortress Wall. The remains of this fortress may not look like much now, but this was the site of an epic battle between the Baekje army and the invading Goryeo forces. Although Baekje King Gaero was killed here, it was the first attempt at unifying the Korean

Bukhansanseong fortress.

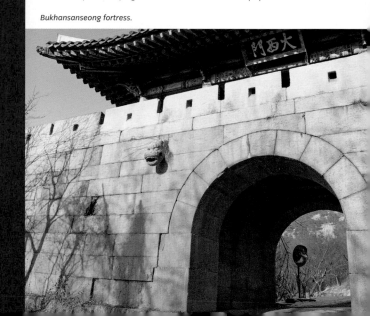

The three main peaks at Bukhansan.

park, it starts at Bukhansanseong hiking support center (they have maps there, but only in Korean) and leads to the highest peak, Baegundae. At the fork in the road you can take either fork, since both merge at Daeseomun (the "Great West Gate"). When you pass Bukhan Village, you'll see a trail that leads to Borisa, the temple. This is where the real trail starts, which runs over 2 miles (3.4km) in length. The last part at the top is a bit steep, but there are chains provided for guidance. ⏱ 5 hr. Admission ₩1,500. Subway: Gwanghwamun, line 5 (exit 1), then walk to the front of the Sejeong Cultural Center and take bus no. 156 to Bukhansan.

★★ Dobongsan/Sinseongdae Trail.

The most popular trail on Dobongsan is also the shortest route to Sinseongdae and its three highest peaks—Seoninbong, Manjangbong, and Jaunbong, which has no trails leading up to it. ⏱ 3 hr. Subway: Dobongsan, line 1.

☕ **San Dubu Jip.** One of the best things about hiking in the mountains is a meal afterward, and this local joint will do you well with handmade tofu dishes. *411-1 Dobong 1(il)-dong, Dobong-gu.* ☎ *02/954-1183. Daily 10am–10pm. $–$$.*

Other Parks

★ **Seoul Dream Forest.** Although it's a bit out of the way, this large park has plenty of walking paths, a gallery, a space-age viewing platform (observatory), and even a handful of deer. The Chinese restaurant on-site has good noodles, too. *28-6 Beon-dong, Gangbuk-gu.* ☎ *02/2289-4001. http://dream forest.seoul.go.kr (Korean only). Outdoor spaces open daily, but many facilities closed Mon. Subway: Dolgoji, line 6 (exit 3), and then take bus no. 147; or Mia Samgeori, line 4 (exit 1), and then take bus no. 9 or 11.*

Seoul Forest. A former hunting ground for royalty, this urban "forest" includes five parks on the riverside island of Ttukseom. *685 1-dong, Seongsu 1(il)-ga, Seongdong-gu.* ☎ *02/460-2905. Free admission. Open daily 24 hr. Subway: Ttukseom, line 2 (exit 8).*

★★ **World Cup Park.** A landfill was converted into a park to commemorate the 17th FIFA World Cup in 2002. Popular with in-line skaters, it encompasses five smaller parks. *45-1 Nanjido-gil, Seongsan-dong, Mapo-gu.* ☎ *02/300-5500. http:// worldcuppark.seoul.go.kr (Korean only). Free admission. Open daily 24 hr. Subway: World Cup Stadium, line 6 (exit 6).*

Biking Along the **Han River**

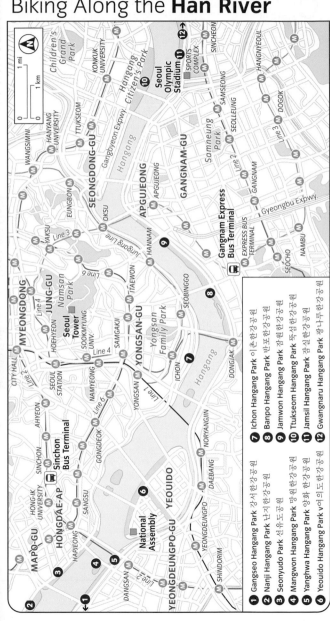

1 Gangseo Hangang Park 강서한강공원
2 Nanji Hangang Park 난지한강공원
3 Seonyudo Park 선유도공원
4 Mangwon Hangang Park 망원한강공원
5 Yanghwa Hangang Park 양화한강공원
6 Yeouido Hangang Park v여의도한강공원
7 Ichon Hangang Park 이촌한강공원
8 Banpo Hangang Park 반포한강공원
9 Jamwon Hangang Park 잠원한강공원
10 Ttukseom Hangang Park 뚝섬한강공원
11 Jamsil Hangang Park 잠실한강공원
12 Gwangnaru Hangang Park 광나루한강공원

One of the best ways to see the city is by two-wheeled pedaler on the many paths along the Han-gang. On the southern side, the path starts around Gwangnaru and runs all the way down to Gangseo Wetland Park. On the northern side, the path goes from Gwangjin Bridge to the Nanji Han River Park. More bike paths are being added every week.

Bike Rentals

Free: Different districts offer a limited number of bikes near some stations. Early birds get the bikes, and there's usually a line on weekends. Rentals limited to 2 hours. Open 9am to 5:30pm daily, except on rainy days. *Jamsil Station (exit 1; ☎ 02/3431-3480); Pungnap-dong (☎ 02/475-4380); Eungbong Station (☎ 02/2293-8111); Oksu Station (☎ 02/2293-8003); Gangbyeon Station (☎ 02/475-4380).*

Paid: There are several locations to rent bikes: one on Jamsil dock (subway: Sincheon, line 2, exit 7), another in Yeouido (subway: Yeouinaru, line 5, under the Wonhyo bridge); others are at Jamwon, Banpo, Yanghwa, Gangseo, Ichon, and Mangwon. You leave your ID or car keys as a deposit. ☎ *02/761-7568. Bike rentals ₩3,000/hr., ₩15,000/day; tandems ₩6,000/hr. Daily 9am–sunset (until 8pm in summer).*

Parks Along the River

All of the parks listed below have numerous biking paths and other facilities. *(Check out http://english.seoul.go.kr/cav/att/hangang.php for more info.)*

Banpo Hangang Park. Known for its rainbow fountain bridge, it's best seen at night during Bangpodaegyo's light-and-water show. *Seocho-gu. ☎ 02/591-5943. Subway: Dongjak, line 4 (exit 1 or 2); or Noksapyeong, line 6 (exit 4), and then take shuttle bus no. 8401.*

Gangseo Hangang Park. Located south of the Haengju Bridge, this is located right next to the Gangseo Wetland Ecological Park, great for seeing migratory birds. *Gaehwa-dong, Gangseo-gu. ☎ 02/3780-0621. Subway: Banghwa, line 5 (exit 1 or 2); then take green bus no. 6.*

Gwangnaru Hangang Park. The only park that has a natural sandy beach, a reed colony, and a nice view of Achasan. ☎ *02/3780-0501. Subway: Cheonho, line 5 or 8 (exit 1) or Amsa, line 8 (exit 4).*

Ichon Hangang Park. It has soccer fields, as well as basketball, volleyball, tennis, and badminton facilities. *Ichon-dong, Yongsan-gu. ☎ 02/3780-0551. Subway: Ichon, line 4 (exit 4).*

kids Jamsil Hangang Park. Near Jamsil Stadium, Lotte World, and Olympic Park, the nature learning center is a good draw for families. *Gangseo-gu. ☎ 02/3780-0511. Subway: Seongnae, line 2 (exit 3 or 4) or Sincheon, line 2 (exit 7).*

Biking at Yeovido Hangang Park.

Ttukseom Hangang Park.

kids Jamwon Hangang Park. With various sports centers and a pool, it also has a silkworm culture learning center that's fun for kids. *Seocho-gu.* ☎ *02/3780-0531. Subway: Sinsa, line 3 (exit 5) or Apgujeong, line 3 (exit 1).*

Mangwon Hangang Park. Between the Wonhyo and Seongsan bridges, you'll find walking trails, a swimming pool, sports fields, and facilities for watersports. *Mapo-gu.* ☎ *02/3780-0601. Subway: Hapjeong, line 2 or 6 (exit 1), and then take bus no. 16; or Mangwon, line 6 (exit 1), and then take bus no. 9.*

Nanji Hangang Park. Located between the Honjecheon and

Yeouido Hangang Park.

Nanjicheon bridges, this park has a baseball field, an archery range, and campsites. It connects to the World Cup Park and Noeul Park. ☎ *02/3780-0612. Subway: Mapo-gu Office Station, line 6 (exit 7) or World Cup Stadium, line 6 (exit 1).*

Seonyudo Park. A water-purification plant turned ecological park and botanical garden. The pump station is now a cafe. ☎ *02/3780-0590. Subway: Dangsan, line 2 or 9 (exit 4).*

Ttukseom Hangang Park. With a waterfront stage, a swimming pool, in-line skating, and a cultural complex, this place is popular in the summer. ☎ *02/3780-0521. Subway: Ttukseom Park, line 7 (exit 2 or 4) or Konkuk Univ., line 2 (exit 3).*

Yanghwa Hangang Park. Stretching from Gayang Bridge to Yeouido bay, the bike lane here is best when the roses are blooming in May. *Yeongdeungpo-gu.* ☎ *02/3780-0581. Subway: Dangsan, line 2 or 9 (exit 4); then take the Dangsan underpass.*

Yeouido Hangang Park. Bike and pedestrian paths surround this island, at its best when the cherry blossoms are in bloom in early spring. They also have a golf course, and in-line skate and boat rentals. *Yeouido.* ☎ *02/3780-0561. Subway: Yeouinaru, line 5 (exit 2 or 3).* ●

Dining Best Bets

Best **Spicy Chicken**
★★ Bongchu Jjimdak $$ *80-1 Myeongnyun-dong 4(sa)-ga, Jongno-gu (p 90)*

Best **Korean Dumplings**
★★★ Jaha Son Mandu $$ *245-2 Buam-dong, Jongno-gu (p 94)*

Best **Tabletop Barbecue**
★★★ Chamsutgol $$$ *2F, 19 Mugyo-dong, Jung-gu (p 91)*

Best **Traditional Korean**
★★★ Yongsusan $$$ *84 Taepyeong-no 1(il)-ga, Jung-gu (p 98)*

Best **Bakery**
★★★ Eric Kayser $ *B1, 60 Yeouido-dong, Yeongdeungpo-gu (p 92)*

Best **Italian**
★★★ The Kitchen Salvatore Cuomo $$$ *646-2 Sinsa-dong, Gangnam-gu (p 95)*

Best **Thai**
★ Zen Hideaway $ *645-18 Sinsa-dong, Gangnam-gu (p 98)*

Best **Middle Eastern Bargain**
★★ Petra Palace $ *552 Itaewon-dong, Yongsan-gu (p 96)*

Best **Celebrity Chef's Joint**
★★★ The Spice $$$$ *729-45 Hannam-dong, Yongsan-gu (p 97)*

Most **Romantic**
★ Top Cloud $$$$$ *1-1 Jongno 2(i)-ga, Jongno-gu (p 98)*

Best **Cafe**
★★★ Tea for Two $ *12-16 Gwancheol-dong, Jongno-gu (p 97)*

Best **Handmade Noodles**
★★ Hyehwa Kalgooksu $ *84-3 Hyehwa-dong, Jongno-gu (p 94)*

Best **Vegetarian**
★★★ Sanchon $$$ *14 Gwanhun-dong, Jung-gu (p 13)*

Best **Royal Cuisine**
★★ Suraon $$$$$ *118-3 Banpo-dong, Seocho-gu (p 97)*

Slurping knife-cut noodles in Myeongdong.

Jongno Dining

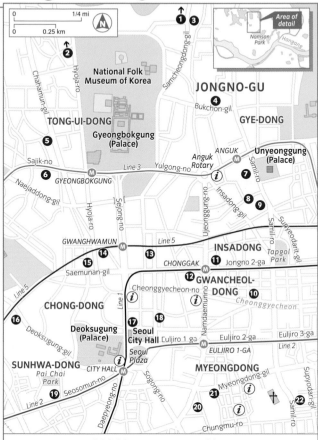

Photo p 83: A spread at Suraon.

Seoul Dining **Best Bets**

Bongchu Jjim Dak 봉추찜닭 **8**

Brooklyn Burger Joint
브루클린 더 버거 조인트 **17**

Chamsutgol 참숯골 **11**

Dalsaeneun Dalman Saengakhanda
달새는달만 생각한다 **14**

Dolggae Maeul Maetdol Soondubu
똘깨마을맷돌순두부 **3**

Eric Kayser 에릭 케제르 **4**

Hyehwa Kalgooksu 혜화칼국수 **9**

Jaha Son Mandu 자하손만두 **1**

Petra Palace 페트라팔레이스 **5**

Samcheonggak 삼청각 **2**

Samwon Garden 삼원가든 **18**

Sanchon 산촌 **15**

Suraon 수라온 **16**

Tea for Two 티포투 **13**

The Kitchen Salvatore Cuomo **19**

The Parkview at the Shilla **7**

The Spice 더스파이스 **6**

Top Cloud 탑클라우드 **12**

Yongsusan 용수산 **10**

Zen Hideaway 젠 하이드어웨이 **20**

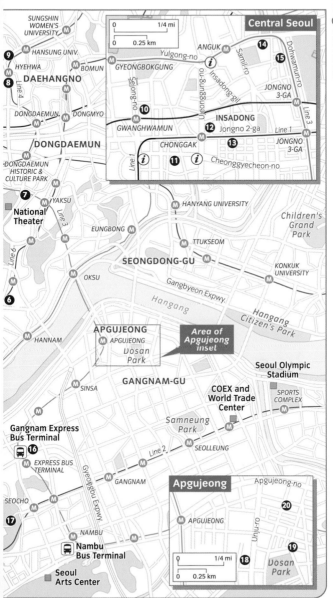

Samcheong-dong Dining

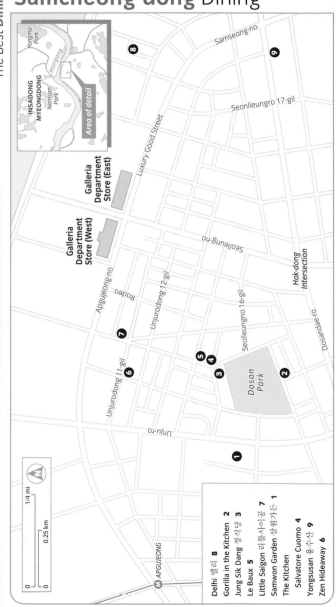

INSADONG
MYEONGDONG

Yongma Park

Hangang

Namsan Park

Area of detail

Samseong-no

Seonlleungro 17-gil

Luxury Good Street

Galleria Department Store (East)

Galleria Department Store (West)

Seolleung-no

Apgujeong-no

Rodeo

Unjurodong 12-gil

Seolleungno 16-gil

Hak-dong Intersection

Dosandae-ro

Unjurodong 11-gil

Dosan Park

Unju-ro

APGUJEONG

1/4 mil

0.25 km

Delhi 델리 **8**
Gorilla in the Kitchen **2**
Jung Sik Dang 정식당 **3**
Le Baux **5**
Little Saigon 리틀사이공 **7**
Samwon Garden 삼원가든 **1**
The Kitchen
Salvatore Cuomo **4**
Yongsusan 용수산 **9**
Zen Hideaway **6**

Daehangno Dining

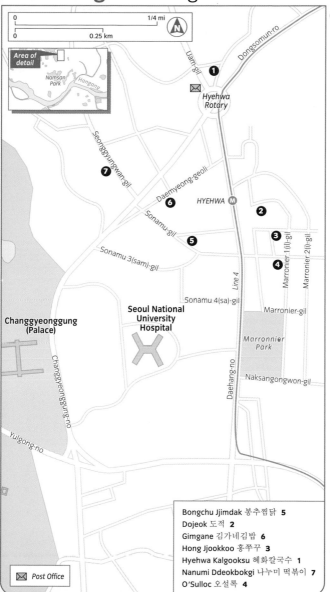

Bongchu Jjimdak 봉추찜닭 **5**
Dojeok 도적 **2**
Gimgane 김가네김밥 **6**
Hong Jjookkoo 홍쭈꾸 **3**
Hyehwa Kalgooksu 혜화칼국수 **1**
Nanumi Ddeokbokgi 나누미 떡볶이 **7**
O'Sulloc 오설록 **4**

✉ Post Office

Dining A to Z

The specialty at Bongchu Jjimdak.

Allo Paper Garden SINSA-DONG *ITALIAN* Tucked in an alley behind Buchella off Garosu-gil, this is a popular spot for weekend brunches. The best thing on the menu is the pasta dishes. *653-11 Sinsa-dong, Gangnam-gu.* ☎ *02/3443-8880. www.papergarden.co.kr. Main courses ₩12,000 and up. MC,V. Cafe daily 11am–1am, hall daily until 11pm. Subway: Sinsa, line 3 (exit 8).*

★ **Baekje Samgyetang** MYEONG-DONG *KOREAN CHICKEN* A great place to get *samgyetang,* the stuffed-chicken soup that's eaten during the 3 hottest days of summer (though it's lovely in the winter as well). The chefs here use only young chickens. Order some *insamju* (ginseng wine) to wash it all down. *50-11 Myeongdong 2(i)-ga, Jung-gu.* ☎ *02/776-3267. No reservations. Main courses ₩11,000 and up. No credit cards. Daily 9am–10pm. Subway: Myeongdong, line 4 (exit 2). Map p 85.*

Bibigo JONGNO *KOREAN* South Korean conglomerate CJ Food's attempt at popularizing *bibimbap* (mixed rice bowl). Its varieties are modern and great for vegetarians. The upstairs sit-down space has a slightly different, more expensive menu. *163 Sinmunno 1(il)-ga, Jongno-gu.* ☎ *02/730-7423. www.ibibigo. com (Korean only). Main courses*

₩7,500 and up. MC, V. Daily 11am–11pm. Subway: Gwanghwamun, line 5 (exit 6). Map p 85.*

★★ **Bongchu Jjimdak** DAE-HANGNO *KOREAN CHICKEN* The soy-steamed chicken may not look spicy, but it's the kind of heat that builds up and won't let go. Bring a friend and share a small order for two. There are many other locations. *80-1 Myeongnyun-dong 4(sa)-ga, Jongno-gu.* ☎ *02/745-6981. www. bongchu.co.kr (Korean only). Main course for 2 ₩20,000 and up. Subway: Hyehwa, line 4 (exit 3). Map p 86 and 89.*

★★ **Brooklyn Burger Joint** SEO-CHO *BURGERS* The battle for the best burger in Seoul has been raging quietly for the past couple of years. Some swear this joint in the Seorae French Village has won—for now. Unadorned meat sits on a perfect sesame bun with your choice of accoutrements. *551-32 Banpo-dong, Seocho-gu.* ☎ *02/533-7180. Main courses ₩8,000 and up. Subway: Express Bus Terminal, line 3 or 7 (exit 5). Map p 86.*

★★ **Buchella** HONGDAE-AP *CAFE* A cozy place to get a sandwich or a cup of coffee and a pastry, while enjoying works by local artists. It has three floors, each with its own different atmosphere, and freshly made sandwiches on ciabattas. There's a smaller location on Garosu-gil. *330-19 Seogyo-dong, Mapo-gu.* ☎ *02/334-7334. Sandwiches ₩8,000 and up. V, MC. Daily 11am–10pm. Subway: Hongik Univ., line 2 (exit 4).*

★★ **Byeokje Galbi** BANGI-DONG *KOREAN BARBECUE* The owners have a farm where the cows graze in the open pastures of Pocheon, in the northeast. You can cook that fresh meat on a tabletop grill and cool off with a bowl of Pyeongang *naengmyeon* (cold buckwheat noodles). *205-8 Bangi-dong, Songpa-gu.* ☎ *02/415-5522. Main courses ₩45,000 and up. AE, MC, V. Daily 11:30am–10pm. Subway: Bangi, line 4 (exit 4).*

★ **Cha Iagi** INSADONG *KOREAN* Don't be fooled by the name, which means "tea story." This spot is actually known for its delicious *nokcha daenamu tongbap* (rice and green tea steamed in bamboo). The *ssambap jeongshik* (meal with lettuce and other leaves for wrapping) isn't bad either. *Insadong 5-gil, Jongno-gu.* ☎ *02/735-8552. No reservations. Main courses ₩7,000 and up. No credit cards. Daily 10am–10pm. Subway: Anguk, line 3 (exit 6).*

★★★ **Chamsutgol** JONGNO *KOREAN BEEF* No one comes for the decor, rather for the tender *galbi* (short ribs) cooked over a real *sutbul* (wood charcoal fire). One of the signature dishes is the *galbitang* (stewed beef ribs), but come early since only 40 servings are made daily. *2F, 19 Mugyo-dong (Chaeyuk Hwaegwan Bldg.), Jung-gu.* ☎ *02/774-2100. Main courses ₩20,000 and up. MC, V. Daily 11:30am–10pm. Subway: City Hall, line 1 (exit 4). Map p 85.*

★★ **Chez Simon** SAMCHEONG-DONG *FRENCH* The former chef of the Park Hyatt, Shim Soonchul,

A street vendor cooking tasty snacks.

serves up delicious courses at this reservation-only restaurant. *63-10 Samcheong-dongJongno-gu.* ☎*02/730-1045. Main courses ₩40,000 and up (prix-fixe only). Daily noon–9:30pm. Subway: Anguk, line 3 (exit 1). Map p 85.*

★★ **Dalmont de Café** GANGNAM *ITALIAN* A casual place for a sandwich, pasta, or one of the best cups of coffee in town. *82-15 Nonhyeon-dong, Gangnam-gu.* ☎ *070/8830-2514. Main courses ₩8,000 and up. Subway: Hakdong, line 7 (exit 9).*

Delhi APGUJEONG *INDIAN* The original location on Rodeo Street was one of the first Indian places in South Korea. You can still get its signature curries and pilau rice here, and at

What's in Those Little Dishes?

One of the fun aspects of a Korean meal is all the little side dishes *(mit banchan)* that come with your rice. There will always be at least one *kimchi* (pickled vegetables), if not two or three seasonal varieties. There may also be some pickled seafood *(jjang-aji),* a seasonal/local vegetable *(namul),* some sheets of seaweed *(laver),* and maybe even some potato salad. Try them all, and if you really like any of them, the waitstaff will always provide refills.

Brunch at Egg and Spoon Race.

five other locations. *2F, 660-18 Sinsa-dong, Gangnam-gu.* ☎ *02/545-7545. www.delhi.co.kr (Korean only). Main courses ₩10,000 and up. AE, MC, V. Daily 10am–10pm. Subway: Apgu-jeong, line 3 (exit 2). Map p 88.*

★ **Din Tai Fung** MYEONGDONG TAIWANESE In this small, stream-lined spot, you'll find a full menu of dumplings, soup, noodles, and rice dishes, but the most popular is the juicy pork dumplings. *104 Myeong-dong 2(i)-ga, Jung-gu.* ☎ *02/771-2778. www.dintaifung.co.kr (Korean only). Main courses ₩5,000 and up. AE, MC, V. Daily 11am–10:30pm. Subway: Myeongdong, line 4 (exit 5). Map p 85.*

★★ **Dojeok** DAEHANGNO KOREAN PORK The spicy *samgyeopssal* (sliced pork belly) brings in the crowds. *2F, 1-47 Dongsung-dong, Jongno-gu.* ☎ *02/743-1011. Main courses ₩9,000 and up. Daily mid-night–2am. Subway: Hyehwa, line 4 (exit 1). Map p 89.*

★★ **Dolggae Maeul Maetdol Soondubu** SINCHON KOREAN If you're looking for bubbling-hot silken tofu in a stone pot, look no further than this place, popular with college kids. *57-7 Changcheon-dong, Seodae-mun-gu.* ☎ *02/338-1722. Main courses ₩6,000 and up. Open daily 24 hr. Subway: Sinchon, line 2 (exit 1 or 2). Map p 86.*

★★ **Eddy's Cafe** GANGNAM WESTERN Celebrity chef Edward Kwon's bistro serves expertly pre-pared sandwiches, salads, and pas-tas in a modern setting. The menu changes bimonthly. *B1, 19-3 Banpo-dong (Shinsegae department store), Seocho-gu.* ☎ *02/3479-1690. Main courses ₩10,000 and up. Mon–Thurs 10am–10pm; Fri–Sun 10am–10:30pm. Subway: Express Bus Terminal, line 3 or 7.*

★★ **Egg and Spoon Race** EDAE-AP CAFE One of the best places in town to brunch, this charming joint has only seven tables beneath a suspended bicycle wheel and hang-ing cutlery. *54-9 Daehyeon-dong, Seodaemun-gu.* ☎ *02/312-5234. Main courses ₩8,000 and up. Sub-way: Ewha Univ., line 2 (exit 3).*

★★★ **Eric Kayser** YEOUIDO BAK-ERY One of Paris's best bakers has set up shop in the 63 building. Crusty baguettes, buttery *pain au chocolat,* and raspberry *financiers* await. *B1, 60 Yeouido-dong, Yeong-deungpo-gu.* ☎ *02/789-5687. www.erickayser.co.kr (mostly Korean). Main courses ₩3,000 and up. Daily 8am–10pm. Subway: Yeouido, line 5 or 9 (exit 2). Map p 86.*

★ **The Flying Pan Blue** ITAE-WON CAFE It used to be difficult to get a good breakfast in Seoul, let

Modern fare at Jung Sik Dang.

Tea at O'Sulloc.

alone all day. Yet this little cafe run by two sisters offered one of the first. Their pancakes are fluffy delights, and their lunch specials great bargains. *127-3 Itaewon-dong, Yongsan-gu.* ☎ *02/793-5285. Main courses ₩8,000 and up. Subway: Itaewon, line 6 (exit 2).*

★ **Ganga** JONGNO *INDIAN* On the second basement floor of the Seoul Finance Center building, it serves wonderful garlic naan, fragrant tandoori dishes, and curries that will make you think you're in Mumbai. *B2, 84 Taepyeong-no 1(il)-ga, Jung-gu.* ☎ *02/3783-0610. Main courses ₩15,000 and up. AE, DC, MC, V. Daily 11:30am–3pm and 5:30–10pm. Subway: Gwanghwamun, line 5 (exit 5) or City Hall, line 1 (exit 4). Map p 85.*

Gimgane DAEHANGNO *KOREAN* Stop in for a snack or make a meal out of the inexpensive *gimbap* (rice rolled in seaweed). Several other locations. *183-1 Myeongnyun-dong 4(sa)-ga, Jongno-gu.* ☎ *02/742-8292. www.gimgane.co.kr. Main courses ₩2,500 and up. Subway: Hyehwa, line 4 (exit 3). Map p 89.*

Gooknae Ddeokbokgi HONGDAE *KOREAN* This snack-food joint does a brisk business. Patrons choose from the limited menu and line up for to-go orders. The few tables have a fast turnaround, so the wait is never long. *486 Seogeo-dong, Mapo-gu.*

☎ *02/322-6124. Main courses ₩2,500 and up. Subway: Hongik Univ., line 2 (exit 4).*

★★ **Gorilla in the Kitchen** APGUJEONG *FUSION* Enjoy healthy sandwiches with sesame soy milk or homemade berry ice cream at this "well-being" restaurant. *650 Sinsa-dong, Gangnam-gu.* ☎ *02/3442-1688. Main courses ₩12,000 and up. AE, MC, V. Daily 11am–11pm (from 10am on weekends). Subway: Apgujeong, line 3 (exit 3). Map p 88.*

Gwanghwamun Jip INSADONG *TEAHOUSE* Lovers of cheap *gimchi jjigae* (kimchi stew) crowd into this tiny hole-in-the-wall. *43 Dangju-dong, Jongno-gu.* ☎ *02/739-7737. Main courses ₩5,000 and up. No credit cards. Daily 9am–10pm. Subway: Gwanghwamun, line 5 (exit 8). Map p 85.*

★★ **Hong Jjookkoo** DAEHANGNO *KOREAN* Super-crowded on weekends, this spot serves a delicious, but affordable, array of meats and seafood for your cook-your-own pleasure. *1-66 Dongsung-dong, Jongno-gu.* ☎ *02/747-3779. Main courses ₩9,000 and up. Daily noon–2am. Subway: Hyehwa, line 4 (exit 2). Map p 89.*

The Parkview.

Passion 5.

★★ **Hyehwa Kalgooksu** DAE-HANGNO *KOREAN NOODLES* Fill up on a hot bowl of *kal guksu* (hand-made noodles) or share a *nokdu buchingae* (mungbean flatcake) with a friend. *84-3 Hyehwa-dong, Jongno-gu. ☎ 02/743-8212. Main courses ₩7,000 and up. Daily 11am–10pm. Subway: Hyehwa, line 4 (exit 4). Map p 89.*

Ipanema JONGNO *BRAZILIAN* The waitstaff cooks tableside at this haven for meat lovers. There are other things on the menu, but it's difficult to resist the churrascaria. *27-11 Jeong-dong, Jongno-gu. ☎ 02/779-2756. Main courses ₩15,000 and up. AE, MC, V. Daily 11:30am–3pm and 5:30–10pm. Subway: Seodaemun, line 5 (exit 5). Map p 85.*

★★★ **Jaha Son Mandu** BUAM-DONG *KOREAN DUMPLINGS* A variety of handmade *mandu* (dumplings) are boiled, put in soups, or just simply steamed. There's another location in Myeongdong's Shin-segae. *245-2 Buam-dong, Jongno-gu. ☎ 02/379-2648. www.sonmandoo. com (Korean only). Main courses ₩10,000 and up. MC, V. Daily 11am–10:30pm. Subway: Gyeongbokgung, line 3 (exit 3). Map p 85.*

★★ **Jangchu** JONGNO *KOREAN SEA-FOOD* For 3 decades, it's been serving *jang-uh gul* (grilled eel) with a

secret ingredient: cinnamon. Look for the squat brick building with a cartoon eel wearing a chef's hat. *58-8 Chungmuro 3(sam)-ga, Jung-gu. ☎ 02/2274-8992. Main courses ₩13,000 and up. MC, V. Daily 11:30am–10pm. Subway: Chungmuro, line 3 or 4 (exit 5). Map p 85.*

★ **Jinokhwa Halmae Wonjo Darhanmari** JONGNO *KOREAN CHICKEN* Located in "One Chicken Alley" (p 32), this is one of the best places to enjoy whole chicken in a pot. *265-22 Jongno 5(o)-ga, Jongno-gu. ☎ 02/2275-9666. www.wonjo dark.co.kr. Main courses ₩20,000 and up. Daily 10am–10:30pm. Subway: Jongno 5(o)-ga, line 1 (exit 5).*

★★ **Jung Sik Dang** APGUJEONG *KOREAN* Playful, nouveau cuisine prepared by a CIA-trained chef. The prix-fixe menu changes every 2 months. *3F, 649-7 Sinsa-dong, Gang-nam-gu. ☎ 02/517-4654. http://jung sikdang.com. Lunch ₩40,000, dinner ₩100,000. Mon–Sat noon–4pm and 6pm–midnight or later; Sun noon–4pm. AE, DISC, MC, V. Subway: Apgu-jeong, line 3 (exit 2). Map p 88.*

★★ **Korea Samgyetang** JUNG-GU *KOREAN CHICKEN* Known for whole chicken soups, this spot stuffs the young birds with special ginseng, sticky rice, chestnuts, dried

Bread and pastries at Paul.

dates, and plenty of garlic. Although a wonderful dish for the cold winters, *samgyetang* is traditionally eaten during the 3 hottest days of summer to fight the heat. *55-3 Seosomun-dong, Jung-gu. ☎ 02/752-9376. Main courses ₩12,000 and up. Daily 10am–9:30pm. Subway: City Hall, line 1 or 2 (exit 10). Map p 85.*

★★★ The Kitchen Salvatore Cuomo APGUJEONG *ITALIAN*

Authentic thin pizza is served from a wood-fired oven. Dine on the terrace and you'll almost swear you're in Napoli. *646-2 Sinsa-dong, Gangnam-gu. ☎ 02/3447-0071. www. kitchensalvatore.kr. Main courses ₩21,000 and up. Daily 11:30am–11pm. Subway: Apgujeong, line 3 (exit 2). Map p 86.*

★ La Celtique SINCHON *FRENCH*

A bit of Bretagne in Seoul, the cheerful creperie is a popular spot with the area's university students. *2F, 5-10 Changcheon-dong, Seodaemungu. ☎ 02/312-7774. Daily 11am–10:30pm. Main courses ₩8,000 and up. Subway: Sinchon, line 2 (exit 2).*

★ Les Baux APGUJEONG *FRENCH*

Real crepes and a wine cellar add to the Provençal charm of this cozy bistro. *642-26 Sinsa-dong, Gangnam-gu. ☎ 02/3444-4226. Daily 11am–2am. Main courses ₩10,000 and up. AE, MC, V. Subway: Apgujeong, line 3 (exit 2). Map p 88.*

Little Saigon APGUJEONG *VIETNAMESE*

Although pho joints are now pretty common, this was one of the first in Seoul to serve the steaming hot noodle bowls. *640-1 Sinsadong, Gangnam-gu. ☎ 02/547-9050. Main courses ₩8,000 and up. MC, V. Mon–Fri 11:40am–5pm; Sat–Sun 11:40am–10pm. Subway: Apgujeong, line 3 (exit 2). Map p 88.*

★ Little Terrace HONGDAE *ITALIAN*

With its fifth-floor vantage point, this wine bar affords some fun

Red Mango's famous frozen yogurt.

views of the action below. *5F, 364-4 Seogyo-dong, Mapo-gu. ☎ 02/333-3310. Main courses ₩10,000 and up. Daily 5pm–2am. Subway: Hongik Univ., line 2 (exit 5).*

Mirinae Makguksu JONGNO *KOREAN*

Although the name of the restaurant says noodles, it also serves an affordable *ssambap* (rice with lettuce and other leaves), since 1969. *27-11 Jung-dong, Jongno-gu. ☎ 02/779-2756. Main courses ₩6,000 and up. MC, V. Tues–Sat 11am–1am. Subway: Gwanghwamun, line 5 (exit 8). Map p 85.*

★ Nanumi Ddeokbokgi DAEHANGNO *KOREAN*

College kids love the cheap and tasty *ddeokbokgi* at this 24-hour joint. This chain restaurant has locations in other areas of the city as well. *225*

Samwon Garden.

Myeongnyun-dong 2(i)-ga, Jongno-gu. ☎ 02/747-0881. Main courses ₩2,500 and up. Subway: Hyehwa, line 4 (exit 4). Map p 89.

★ Nanxiang Steamed Bun

JONGNO *CHINESE DUMPLINGS* At Shanghai's famous bun shop, try one of the signature pork, chicken and ginseng, or pork and pine mushroom dumplings. *84 Taepyeong-no 1-ga, Jongno-gu.* ☎ 02/3789-8074. Main courses ₩8,000 and up. MC, V. Daily 11am–10pm. Subway: City Hall, line 1 (exit 5).

N'Grill JONGNO *WESTERN*

Perched on top of the N Seoul Tower on Namsan, it's a romantic place to enjoy an overpriced steak while enjoying the city lights as the place spins 360 degrees every 48 minutes. Book a reservation well in advance and hope for a clear night. *100-177 Hoehyeon-dong 1-ga, Jung-gu.* ☎ 02/753-2563. www.nseoultower. co.kr. Reservations required. Set menus ₩55,000 and up. AE, MC, V. Daily 11am–11pm. Subway: Myeong-dong, line 4 (exit 2 or 3); then take cable car or yellow bus no. 02.

★ O'Sulloc DAEHANGNO *TEA-HOUSE* A modern place to get a snack and drink, it specializes in green tea but has a pretty wide selection. *1F, 1-104 Dongsung-dong, Jongno-gu.* ☎ 02/741-5461. www. osulloc.com. Teas ₩5,000 and up.

A performance at Suraon.

Daily 11am–11pm. Subway: Hyehwa, line 4 (exit 2). Map p 89.

★★ The Parkview JUNG-GU

FUSION Inside the Shilla hotel, the king crab legs bring in diners for the weekend buffet. The well-presented mix of Asian and Western flavors is almost worth the dent in your wallet. *202 Jangchung-dong 2(i)-ga, Jung-gu.* ☎ 02/2230-3374. www. shilla.net. Buffet ₩60,000 and up. Subway: Dongguk Univ., line 3 (exit 5). Map p 86.

★ Passion 5 HANNAM-DONG *BAK-ERY CAFE* Choose a creamy pudding or inventive pastry downstairs, and then head upstairs to the hipper-than-thou cafe whose service leaves a lot to be desired. Nice for a stop after a visit to the Leeum Samsung Museum. *729-74 Hannam-dong, Yongsan-gu.* ☎ 02/2071-9505. Main courses ₩5,000 and up. Daily 7:30am–9pm. Subway: Hangangjin, line 6 (exit 3).

★ Paul YEOUIDO *BAKERY CAFE*

The chandeliers, curtains, placemats, and even the servers' uniforms here were all imported. This Parisian favorite now serves overpriced sandwiches and pastries in a gorgeous dining room in the Marriott. *28-3 Yeouido-dong, Yeong-deungpo-gu.* ☎ 02/2070-3000. www.paulkorea.com. Main courses ₩15,000 and up. Daily 8am–10pm. Subway: Yeouido, line 5 or 9 (exit 2).

★★ Petra Palace ITAEWON *MID-DLE EASTERN* Located right on the main drag, the little sister of a local favorite serves up some righteous kebabs and falafels in a fast-food setting. Even the fries are delicious. Go to the main location for a larger menu and some "hubbly bubbly" (as hookah is known in Jordan). *552 Itae-won-dong, Yongsan-gu.* ☎ 02/790-4433. www.petrakorea.com. Main courses ₩5,000 and up. Subway: Itaewon, line 6 (exit 2). Map p 86.

★ **Red Mango** GANGAM *DESSERT* This is the chain that started the South Korean frozen yogurt craze. Choose from a variety of toppings, or share a yogurt *bingsu* (shaved-ice dessert) with a friend. *2F, 1305-7 Seocho-dong, Seocho-gu. ☎ 02/3476-5582. ₩3,000 and up. Daily 10am–10:30pm. Subway: Gangnam, line 2 (exit 6).*

★ **Samarkand** DONGDAEMUN *UZBEKISTANI* Be transported to the old country with the *gostovy* (cabbage stuffed with lamb) and other stick-to-your-ribs fare. *54 Gwanghui-dong 1(il)-ga, Jung-gu. ☎ 02/2277-4261. www.samarikant. com (Korean only). Main courses ₩10,000 and up. Daily 9am–11pm. Subway: Dongdaemun History & Culture Park, line 2 (exit 12).*

★★★ **Samwon Garden** APGUJEONG *KOREAN* Since 1976, Samwon Garden has served its famous galbi in this gigantic space. The garden is perfect during good weather. There is another location in Daechidong. *623-5 Sinsa-dong, Gangnam-gu. ☎ 02/548-3030. www.samwon garden.com. Main courses ₩25,000 and up. AE, DC, MC, V. Daily 11:40am–10pm. Subway: Apgujeong, line 3 (exit 2). Map p 86.*

★ **Siena** GANGNAM *ITALIAN* Pizza and pasta joints are a dime a dozen, but very few deliver with both atmosphere and food like this one. A relaxing place for a thin-crust pizza and a glass of wine. *928-23 Daechi 4(sa)-dong, Gangnam-gu. ☎ 02/568-0948. Main courses ₩25,000 and up. MC, V. Daily noon–10pm. Subway: Apgujeong, line 3 (exit 2).*

★★★ **The Spice** HANNAM-DONG *WESTERN* Celebrated chef Edward Kwon serves delicious modern fare in a clublike setting—music and disco balls included. *729-45 Hannam-dong, Yongsan-gu.*

A dish at Wood & Brick.

☎ 02/749-2596. Main courses ₩27,500 and up. Daily 11:30am–2am. Subway: Hangangjin, line 6 (exit 3). Map p 86.

★★ **Suraon** SEOCHO *KOREAN* Be treated like a king or queen at this special-occasion restaurant that serves multicourse royal meals complete with performances. *118-3 Banpo-dong, Seocho-gu. ☎ 02/595-0202. www.suraon.co.kr (Korean only). Set menus ₩35,000 and up. Subway: Express Bus Terminal, line 3 (exit 2) or line 7 (exit 3). Map p 86.*

★★★ **Tea for Two (T42)** JONGNO *CAFE* A multistoried cafe in the middle of the city, it often has live concerts and other events. *12-16 Gwancheol-dong, Jongno-gu. ☎ 02/735-5437. www.t42.co.kr (Korean only). Drinks ₩7,000 and up. Subway: Jonggak, line 1 (exit 4). Map p 85.*

Tomatillo JONGNO *MEXICAN* Build your own taco or burrito at this affordable Mexican joint. It has fresh ingredients, but no tomatillos, as the name would suggest. *1F, 70 Seorin-dong (Alpha Bldg.), Jongno-gu. ☎ 02/734-9225. www.tomatillo. co.kr (Korean only). Main courses ₩3,800 and up. Mon–Fri 7:30am–10pm; Sat–Sun 11am–10pm. Subway: Jonggak, line 1 (exit 6). Map p 85.*

Navigating Street Food

Every street in Seoul is filled with carts and vendors that sell food. You'll see well-heeled ladies and men in business suits chowing down next to teenagers under covered tents *(pojang macha)*. Some of the tastiest options are *hoddeok* (pan-fried dough cakes stuffed with brown sugar and cinnamon), *gimbap* (rice rolled in sheets of seaweed with a variety of different fillings), and *ddeokbokgi* (rice cake sticks in a spicy red sauce). Colder weather brings fresh roasted chestnuts, while the summers are filled with steamed corn on the cob and other hot-weather crops. The best places to find good street food are near Namdaemun or Dongdaemun markets, in Myeongdong, and on Insadong-gil.

★ **Top Cloud** JONGNO *WESTERN* Run by the Shilla Hotel, this elegant restaurant is perfect for a romantic night out. Be sure to request a window seat for the view. Overpriced cocktails in the bar with live jazz daily 7:30 to 11:30pm. *33F, 1-1 Jongno 2(i)-ga (Jongno Tower), Jongno-gu.* ☎ *02/2230-3000. www. topcloud.co.kr. Reservations recommended. Lunch set ₩45,000, dinner set ₩65,000. AE, DC, MC, V. Daily noon–2:30pm and 6–10pm. Bar daily noon–midnight. Subway: Jonggak, line 1 (exit 3). Map p 85.*

Walking on the Cloud YEOUIDO *WESTERN* On the 59th floor of the 63 City building (p 118), couples get engaged while sipping on wine and eating Koreanized steak dishes. *60 Yeouido-dong, Yeongdeungpo-gu.* ☎ *02/789-6114. Main courses ₩30,000 and up. Daily 11:30am–3:30pm and 5:30–10pm. Wine bar daily 11:30am–2am. Subway: Yeouinaru, line 5 (exit 4); then take free shuttle.*

★★ **Wood & Brick** JONGNO *ITALIAN* Come here for fantastic pastas, sandwiches, soups, and excellent pastries. Upstairs is more formal, while the downstairs bakery offers a more casual meal. There are a couple of other locations. *5-2 Jae-dong, Jongno-gu.* ☎ *02/747-1592. www.woodnbrick.co.kr. Main courses ₩25,000 and up. MC, V. Daily noon–10pm. Subway: Anguk, line 3 (exit 1 or 2). Map p 85.*

★★★ **Yongsusan** Although it has other locations, this stylish space in the financial district is the original. Enjoy a multicourse meal or a healthy bibimbap. *B1, 84 Taepyeong-no 1(il)-ga (Seoul Finance Center Bldg.), Jung-gu.* ☎ *02/771-5553. www.yongsusan.co.kr. Main courses ₩28,000 and up. Subway: City Hall, line 1 or 2 (exit 4) or Gwanghwamun, line 5 (exit 5) Map p 85.*

★ **Zen Hideaway** APGUJEONG *THAI FUSION* The indoor garden, complete with running water, and the wine list bring in the beautiful people. The well-portioned dishes are good to share. *645-18 Sinsa-dong, Gangnam-gu.* ☎ *02/541-1461. Main courses ₩16,000 and up. Daily 11:30am–2am. Subway: Sinsadong, line 3 (exit 1). Map p 86.* ●

The Best Nightlife

Nightlife Best Bets

Best Cocktail Bar
★★★ Coffee Bar K, 89-20
Cheongdam-dong, Gangnam-gu.
(p 107)

Best DJs
★★★ Mix Lounge, 532-4 Sinsa-
dong, Gangnam-gu (p 106)

Best Makgeolli (Milky Rice
Wine) Bar
★★★ Moon Jar, 644-19 Sinsa-dong,
Gangnam-gu. (p 111)

Best Hookah Lounge
★★★ Rainbow Hookah Lounge,
B1, 1308-11 Seocho-dong, Seocho-gu
(p 109)

Best Wine Bar
★★★ Naos Nova, 448-120 Huam-
dong, Yongsan-gu (p 112)

Best View & Cocktails
★★ Sky Lounge, 159 Samseong-
dong, Gangnam-gu (p 107)

Best Brewpub
★★ Castle Praha, B2, 1306-6-beonji
Seocho-dong, Seocho-gu (p 106)

Best Gay Bar
★★ Bar Bliss, 72-32 Itaewon-dong,
Yongsan-gu (p 108)

Best Live Jazz
★★★ All That Jazz, 168-17 Itaewon-
dong, Yongsan-gu (p 109)

Best Neighborhood Pub
★★ 3 Alley Pub, 116-15 Itaewon-
dong, Yongsan-gu (p 112)

Best Drinks to Go
★ Vinyl, 411-1 Seogyo-dong,
Mapo-gu (p 106)

Best Noraebang (Private
Karaoke)
★★★ Prince Edward, 364-24
Seogyo-dong, Mapo-gu (p 110)

Best Dance Club
★★★ Club M2, 367-11 Seogyo-
dong, Mapo-gu (p 107)

Best Club Parties
★★★ Mansion, 368-22 Seogyo-
dong, Mapo-gu (p 108)

Best Live Rock Club
★★ Club FF, 407-8 Seogyo-dong,
Mapo-gu (p 110)

Bar Bliss.

Itaewon Nightlife

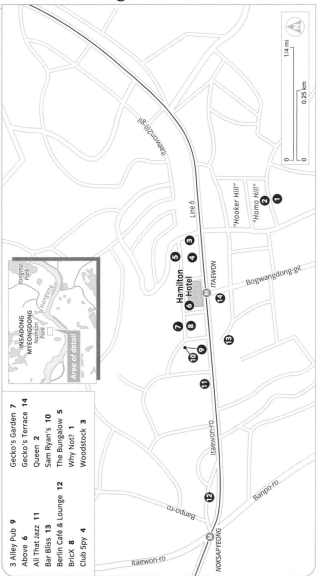

3 Alley Pub **9**
Above **6**
All That Jazz **11**
Bar Bliss **13**
Berlin Café & Lounge **12**
BricX **8**
Club Spy **4**
Gecko's Garden **7**
Gecko's Terrace **14**
Queen **2**
Sam Ryan's **10**
The Bungalow **5**
Why Not? **1**
Woodstock **3**

Photo p 99: Seoul street at night.

Seoul Nightlife Best Bets

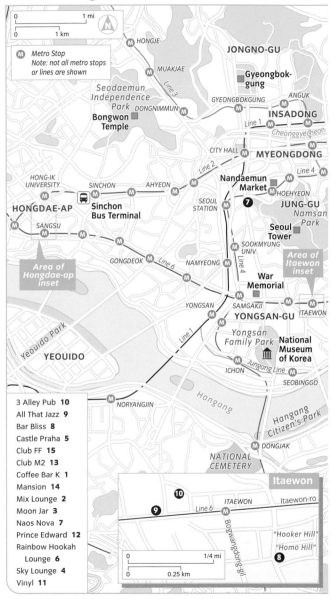

3 Alley Pub **10**
All That Jazz **9**
Bar Bliss **8**
Castle Praha **5**
Club FF **15**
Club M2 **13**
Coffee Bar K **1**
Mansion **14**
Mix Lounge **2**
Moon Jar **3**
Naos Nova **7**
Prince Edward **12**
Rainbow Hookah
  Lounge **6**
Sky Lounge **4**
Vinyl **11**

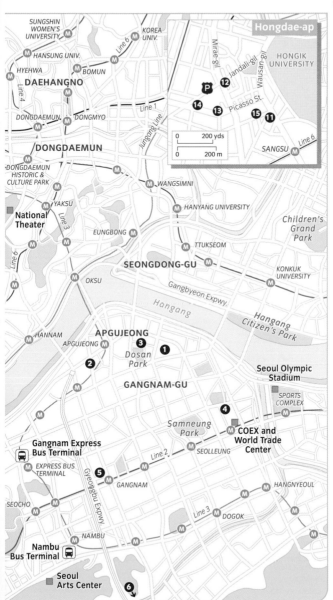

Hongdae Nightlife

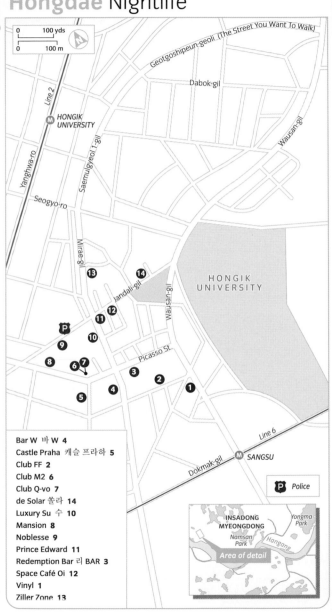

Bar W 바 W **4**

Castle Praha 캐슬 프라하 **5**

Club FF **2**

Club M2 **6**

Club Q-vo **7**

de Solar 쏠라 **14**

Luxury Su 수 **10**

Mansion **8**

Noblesse **9**

Prince Edward **11**

Redemption Bar 리 BAR **3**

Space Café Oi **12**

Vinyl **1**

Ziller Zone **13**

P Police

INSADONG
MYEONGDONG

Namsan
Park

Yongma
Park

Hangang

Area of detail

Cheongdam-dong Nightlife

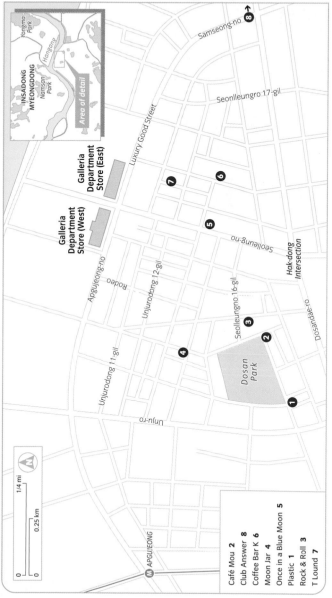

Café Mou **2**
Club Answer **8**
Coffee Bar K **6**
Moon Jar **4**
Once in a Blue Moon **5**
Plastic **1**
Rock & Roll **3**
T Lound **7**

Nightlife A to Z

Drinks served in plastic bags at Vinyl.

Bars

★★★ Blush GANGNAM   Located inside the Grand InterContinental, this sleek and stylish space is designed for a younger crowd. It has a good selection of wines and cocktails in two separate bar areas with plenty of spaces for those seeking more privacy. *521 Teheran-ro, Gangnam-gu.* ☎ *02/559-7619. www.blushbar.co.kr. Closed Sun.*

★★★ Mix Lounge SINSA-DONG This tiny but popular bar, located near Garosu-gil, serves up fabulous mojitos and apple martinis. Squeeze in with your friends to enjoy the house music mixed up by some of the city's best DJs. *532-4 Sinsa-dong (Masa Bldg. no. 103), Gangnam-gu.* ☎ *02/546-4090. http://cafe.naver.com/mixlounge.cafe (Korean only). Closed Sun. Map p 102.*

★ Plastic SINGSA-DONG   The minimalist decor and lovely terrace bring a more professional crowd to this popular cafe and bar in the Dosan Park area. *631-13 Sinsa-dong, Gangnam-gu.* ☎ *02/3446-4646. Map p 105.*

★★ Redemption Bar HONGDAE Called "Re" by regulars, this reggae bar has tiki influences with a touch of the magical mystery tour. A lounge hidden in the basement has comfortable couches, great for kicking back with friends. *405-4 Seogyo-dong, Mapo-gu.* ☎ *02/322-5743. Subway: Hapjeong, line 2 (exit 3). Map p 104.*

★ Vinyl HONGDAE   Only in Seoul can you have a bar where you can order cheap cocktails served in zipper bags from a take-out window. If you can get a seat in the tiny space, you can listen to great music while drinking from your plastic bag. *411-1 Seogyo-dong, Mapo-gu.* ☎ *02/322-4161. Subway: Sangsu. line 6 (exit 1) Map p 102 and 104.*

★★ WooBar WALKER HILL   Step into the future at this 18m (59-ft.) bar lit from below. Sit in one of the dangling egg-shaped chairs or a cabana in the glassed-in mezzanine as you choose from the extensive wine menu. *175 Achaseong-gil, Gwangjin-gu.* ☎ *02/2022-0333.*

Brew Houses

★★ Castle Praha GANGNAM   An excellent place to get an authentic Czech brew and food, it also has locations in Hongdae and Itaewon. *B2, 1306-6-beonji Seocho-dong (Pagoda Tower), Seocho-gu.* ☎ *02/596-9200. www.castlepraha.com (Korean only). Subway: Gangnam, line 2 (exit 6). Map p 102 and 104.*

O'Kim's Brauhaus GANGNAM On the first floor of the COEX Mall, this pub has an on-site brewery and makes three German beers (which change with the seasons). It cranks out a Korean brew and has other imported bottled beers as well. *159 Samseong-dong, Gangnam-gu.*

☎ 02/6002-7006. Subway: Sam-seong, line 2 (exit 5 or 6).

Cafes

★ **Café Mou** SINSA-DONG At this Moroccan-themed hideaway on the edge of Dosan Park, you'll spot couples on blind dates talking over a cup of coffee. *650-9 Sinsa-dong (Park View Bldg.), Gangnam-gu.* ☎ *02/3444-8401. Map p 105.*

★ **Rainbow Café** JAMWON Of the nine cafes built on Han River bridges, this was the first. It's a nice place to have a makgeolli cocktail while enjoying the nighttime view from Hannamdaegyo. *Hannam Bridge.* ☎ *02/511-7345. Subway: Sinsa, line 3 (exit 4).*

Note: See chapter 6, "The Best Dining," for a list of more cafes (most stay open late).

Cocktail Bars

★★★ **Coffee Bar K** CHEONG-DAM-DONG Affectionately called "K Bar" by locals, this Japanese-owned lounge boasts world-class mixologists. Reserve a table to try the selection of single-malt whiskies and Cuban cigars, in addition to the inventive cocktails. *89-20 Cheongdam-dong, Gangnam-gu.* ☎ *02/516-1970. www.coffeebark. co.jp. Subway: Apgujeong, line 3 (exit 1). Map p 102.*

★★ **Sky Lounge** GANGNAM Since it's on the 30th floor of the COEX InterContinental, visitors come for the fabulous views while enjoying well-prepared cocktails or a bite from the European and pan-Asian menu. The live music helps set the mood. *159 Samseong-dong, Gangnam-gu.* ☎ *02/3452-2500. Map p 102.*

★★ **T Lound** CHEONGDAM-DONG Some of the best cocktails in the city, but you'll be paying for the privilege as well as the fabulously

Castle Praha.

swanky glass-and-light interior that spans three stories. *83-13-beonji Cheongdam-dong, Gangnam-gu.* ☎ *02/517-7412. www.74lound.com (Korean only). Subway: Apgujeong, line 3 (exit 1). Map p 105.*

Dance Clubs

★★ **Club Answer** CHEONGDAM-DONG At this club, you can groove to techno beats on the expansive floor. The second-floor tables are great for checking out the action below. *125-16 Cheongdam-dong, Gangnam-gu.* ☎ *02/548-7115. www. clubanswer.co.kr. Map p 105.*

★★★ **Club Eden** GANGNAM Located inside the Ritz-Carlton, this huge and classy dance floor can get pretty packed on weekends. The house DJ spins minimalist techno, but guest DJs can bring the house down. *602 Yeoksam-dong, Gangnam-gu.* ☎ *02/6447 0042. http://club-eden.co.kr (Korean only).*

★★★ **Club M2** HONGDAE Even with three bars and a huge dance floor, it can still get pretty crowded at this popular club known for its high-tech lighting, hip crowds, and its electro parties. *367-11 Seogyo-dong (Ohoo Bldg.), Mapo-gu. ☎ 02/ 3143-7573. www.clubm2.co.kr. Map p 102 and 104.*

★ **Club Q-Vo** HONGDAE Those looking for hip-hop need look no further than this thumping place located above Club M2. The action starts after midnight on party nights. *367-11 Seogyo-dong (Ohoo Bldg.), Mapo-gu. ☎ 02/3143-7573. http://ohoo.net/qvo. Map p 104.*

★ **Club Spy** ITAEWON Popular with expats, the floor starts getting crowded around midnight and the party goes to the early hours. The separate lounge is a perfect place to rest your feet between sets. *123-23 Itaewon 2(i)-dong, Yongsan-gu. ☎ 02/796-9993. Subway: Itaewon, line 6 (exit 2). Map p 101.*

★★★ **Mansion** HONGDAE Legendary for its club parties (friend its Facebook page for the latest). When parties aren't being held here, it becomes a mellow lounge for enjoying drinks in plush settings under low-lit chandeliers. *368-22 Seogyo-dong, Mapo-gu. ☎ 02/3143-4037. Subway: Hongik Univ., line 2 (exit 5). Map p 102 andf 104.*

Gay & Lesbian

★★ **Bar Bliss** ITAEWON At the location of the oldest openly gay bar, Teddy Park offers a "blissful" hour at his inviting and tastefully decorated wine bar. DJs spin Saturdays, and Fridays are drag bingo nights. *72-32 Itaewon-dong, Yongsan-gu. ☎ 02/ 749-7738. http://barblissseoul. wordpress.com. Map p 101 and 102.*

★ **Barcode** JONGNO A classy joint with an international crowd outside of the usual Itaewon digs. The English-speaking owner can fill you in on the city's gay scene. *2F, Myo-dong, Jongno-gu. ☎ 02/3672-0940. Subway: Jongno 3(sam)-ga, line 1, 3, or 5 (exit 3 or 8).*

★★ **Bar W** HONGDAE One of the few relaxed lesbian-friendly joints (all concentrated in the Hongdae area), it features good cocktails and has a tiny area for bumping and grinding. *402-13 Seogyo-dong, Mapo-gu. ☎ 02/3377-117. www.wbar.co.kr (Korean only). Map p 104.*

★★ **Queen** ITAEWON A popular and friendly dance club in the area of Itaewon nicknamed Homo Hill, its popular DJs bring in mixed crowds on weekends. *136-42 Itaewon-dong, Yongsan-gu. ☎ 02/793-1290. Closed Mon. Map p 101.*

Hongdae Club Day

The area in front of Hongik University (aka Hongdae-ap) has the highest concentration of clubs in Seoul. If you happen to be in town the last Friday of the month, don't miss "Club Day" (www. theclubday.co.kr; Korean only). More than 20 clubs get together to throw this monthly party. For only ₩20,000 (about the cost of a cover charge for one club), you get into all of the other participating clubs for free. Your paper bracelet also includes one beer or soft drink from any club. Although it starts at 8pm, the crowds don't come out until 11ish, and the revelry goes on until about 2am. Take subway line 2 to Hongik University (exit 6).

★ **Why Not?** ITAEWON An established gay joint, it has a mixed crowd that packs the dance floor starting at midnight. DJs play American pop and techno, with a bit of house thrown in. *137-4 Itaewon-dong, Yongsan-gu.* ☎ *02/795-8193. Map p 101.*

Hookah Lounges

BricX HANNAM-DONG Although the Itaewon location is more popular with expats, the Hannam-dong location is the main digs. The location in Hongdae also has a good atmosphere. Live DJ on weekends. *3F, 91-5-beonji Hannam-dong, Yongsan-gu.* ☎ *02/3785-1555. www.bricx.com. Map p 101.*

★★★ **Rainbow Hookah Lounge** GANGNAM Once patrons enter this cozy underground joint, they take off their shoes and chill on floor rugs. The hard part is choosing what flavor to smoke from the extensive list. *B1, 1308-11 Seocho-dong, Seocho-gu.* ☎ *02/3481-1869. www.myspace.com/rainbowhookah. Map p 102.*

Jazz Clubs (Live)

★★★ **All That Jazz** ITAEWON The first jazz club in Korea, it's still no-frills in presenting musicians. Live acts start around 9pm, so get there early to snag a table. *168-17 Itaewon-dong, Yongsan-gu.* ☎ *02/795-5701. www.allthatjazz.kr. Map p 101 and 102.*

Cheonnyeondongando DAE-HANG-NO A spot popular with the younger crowd, it holds more than 200 people, but it doesn't have the character of some of the smaller joints. *1-66 Dongsung-dong, Jongno-gu.* ☎ *02/743-5555. www.chunnyun.com (Korean only).*

★ **Jazz Alley** NAKSEONGDAE A newer, more spacious version of Mr. Park's first club **Mo' Better Blues,** some big Korean and international jazz artists play here. *1627-12*

Rainbow Hookah Lounge.

Bongcheon-dong, Gwanak-gu. ☎ *02/882-5545. http://cafe.naver.com/club jazzalley (Korean only).*

★ **Once in a Blue Moon** CHEONG-DAM-DONG This classic jazz club has gotten more upscale and serves fancy hotel fare and cocktails named after musicians. Music 7 and 10pm most nights. *85-1 Cheongdam-dong, Gangnam-gu.* ☎ *02/549-5490. www.onceinabluemoon.co.kr. Map p 105.*

★★ **Solar Jazz** HONGDAE This secret jazz joint (formerly called Watercock) showcases all types of jazz musicians but favors vocalists.

Performance at Once in a Blue Moon.

Singing at a noraebang.

Pyeong-ga, Seogyo-dong, Mapo-gu. ☎ 02/324-2422. www.solarjazz. co.kr.

Karaoke (Noraebang)

★★ **Luxury Su** HONGDAE   One of the many high-end noraebangs, this chain also has locations in Gangnam and other happening areas. Expect to pay higher-than-average prices for the fancy rooms (some with street views), the great service, and the on-site bakery. *367-39 Seogyo-dong, Mapo-gu.* ☎ *02/322-3111. www.skysu.com (Korean only). Map p 104.*

★★★ **Prince Edward** HONGDAE The faux Victorian decor lets you know you're in for a treat at this "luxury" noraebang. If you're a serious belter, you can even book time on the white baby grand in the lobby or get a room with real guitars and drum sets. *364-24 Seogyo-dong, Mapo-gu.* ☎ *02/336-2332. Map p 102 and 104.*

★★ **Ziller Zone** HONGDAE   A hip and happening noraebang that's great for large groups. Each room (Adonis, Hermes, and so on) has its own fun character. *358-114 Seogyo-dong, Mapo-gu.* ☎ *02/338-3531. www.zillerzone.com (Korean only). Map p 104.*

Live Music

★★ **Club FF** HONGDAE   The FF stands for "funky funky" at this basement club. It features local indie bands with a DJ who spins rock, hip-hop, and, of course, funk. *407-8 Seogyo-dong, Mapo-gu.* ☎ *010/6428-0248. Map p 102 and 104.*

★★ **Rock & Roll** SINGSA-DONG An established classic in the area, it features live bands rocking out in a wood-paneled setting. *648-4 Sinsa-dong, Gangnam-gu.* ☎ *02/545-4163. Map p 105.*

Woodstock ITAEWON   Expat bands play classic rock here at around 10pm, while Sunday's open

Private Singing Rooms

Noraebang, which translate to "song room," has been a Korean phenomenon for decades. Private karaoke rooms are perfect for those who fear singing in public, since you belt it out only to your private party. Set up like recording studios, a series of soundproof rooms line both sides of hallways. Each room has a giant screen TV, a couple of microphones, and song books from which you can pick a song by inputting the corresponding number. You can use the phone in the room to order food and drinks (most don't allow alcohol). Rooms start around ₩15,000 per hour, but a luxury norae-bang can cost ₩20,000 and up. Oddly, most of them also provide free ice cream (usually self-serve in the lobby).

mic attracts a mellower crowd. Another location in Sinchon. *19-25 Itaewon-dong, Yongsan-gu.* ☎ *02/ 749-6034. Map p 101.*

Lounges

★★ Berlin Café & Lounge ITAEWON   A mild-mannered bar and restaurant by week, it turns into a lively burlesque joint with live DJs and performers on weekends. The turn-of-the-century art on the walls makes it a cozy place to enjoy a well-made cocktail any day. *457-1 Itaewon-dong, Yongsan-gu.* ☎ *02/ 749-0903. Subway: Noksapyeong, line 6 (exit 3). Map p 101.*

★ The Bungalow ITAEWON This "tropical lounge" complete with fake palm trees and real sand is a mellow place to get a cocktail. The bar spans two floors and has a popular rooftop, all connected by twisting staircases. *112-3 Itaewon-dong, Yongsan-gu.* ☎ *02/793-2344. Map p 101.*

★ Space Café Oi HONGDAE   The space-age decor here comes complete with dangling jellyfish and candlelight. The perfect place to relax with some beers or share a hookah with friends, it transforms into a space for club parties on weekends. *3F, 364-26 Seogyo-dong (CatchLight Bldg.), Mapo-gu.* ☎ *02/334-5484. www.oooooooi.com. Map p 104.*

Makgeolli Bar

★★★ Moon Jar SINSA-DONG   If you can't get makgeolli out in the Korean countryside, the next best place is here. Pour your rice wine from a kettle and enjoy deliciously large *anju* (drinking snacks). *644-19 Sinsa-dong, Gangnam-gu.* ☎ *02/541- 6118. www.moonjar.co.kr (Korean only). Map p 102.*

★ Ssalip Mooneul Mitgo Deuluh Seoni INSADONG   In an alley off the main drag, this traditional house serves a special makgeolli

Space Café Oi.

and a variety of other traditional alcohols in a cozy, warmly lit space. *154-10 Insadong, Jongno-gu.* ☎ *02/ 735-5917.*

Pubs & Sports Bars

★ Gecko's Terrace ITAEWON   It opens early for those looking for some greasy finger food and a beer for lunch, but the action happens after dark. Both this location and its sister, Gecko's Garden, attract expats who come for the relaxed atmosphere. *128-5 Itaewon-dong, Yongsan-gu.* ☎ *02/749-9425. Subway: Itaewon, line 6 (exit 1). Map p 101.*

★ Sam Ryan's ITAEWON   The owners of 3 Alley Pub (see below) run this sports bar upstairs. With eight flatscreen TVs and plenty of beer, it's a sports-lover's dream. *2F, 116-15 Itaewon-dong, Yongsan-gu.* ☎ *02/749-7933. Map p 101.*

Makgeolli at Moon Jar.

153 has an extensive wine list.

★★ **Sir Raymond** SINGSA-DONG An English pub in Seoul? Why not? Don't expect a British owner, but you can still find fish and chips, football on the telly, and plenty of English brews to go around. Located on Sinsa-dong's Garosugil. *547-6 Sinsa-dong, Gangnam-gu.* ☎ *02/516-5476.*

★★ **3 Alley Pub** ITAEWON A congenial neighborhood spot, this bar has a good selection of brews and a European menu. You can battle it out for free beer on quick trivia Thursdays. *116-15 Itaewon-dong, Yongsan-gu.* ☎ *02/749-3336. www.3alleypub.com. Map p101 and 102.*

Watts on Tap SINCHON Owned by a friendly Canadian, you'll find a good selection of beers and an international menu of greasy pub fare. Regulars come for the rooftop terrace and the occasional live show. *3F, 52-84 Changcheon-dong, Seodaemun-gu.* ☎ *02/3142-8439. Subway: Sinchon, line 2 (exit 2).*

Wine Bars

★★ **Above** ITAEWON The upscale Moroccan interior is the perfect place to sip a glass of wine or retire to the cozy candlelit patio on warm nights. *119-25 Itaewon-dong, Yongsan-gu.* ☎ *02/749-0717. Subway: Itaewon, line 6 (exit 3). Map p 101.*

★★ **Bar 153** JONGNO The 153 indicates the number of wines available at this sleek but intimate cocktail lounge. The owner is an excellent sommelier, and the martinis bring loyal fans. *2F, 1-153 Sinmunno 2(i)-ga (The Garden Place), Jongno-gu.* ☎ *02/3210-3351. Subway: Gwanghwamun, line 5 (exit 7).*

★★★ **Naos Nova** HUAM-DONG Choose from three levels—heaven, earth, or hell—to enjoy French fusion dishes and a selection of 200-plus beverages. It has killer views and a hip interior. *448-120 Huam-dong, Yongsan-gu.* ☎ *02/754-2202. www.naosnova.com. Subway: Hoehyeon, line 4 (exit 4). Map p 102.* ●

Drinking Etiquette

Drinking is a communal pastime in Korea. Groups of men in suits, friends gathering after work, or even couples on dates can be seen enjoying everything from jugs of creamy white makgeolli and shots of *soju* (a clear distilled alcohol) to just plain *maekju* (beer). Drinking customs aren't numerous but can be a little complicated. For starters, one should never fill his/her own glass. Koreans pour for each other, holding their glass with both hands if an elder/superior is pouring, or pouring with both hands for an elder/superior. When drinking a soju shot in front of an elder, one should turn away, since it's considered rude to drink in front of them. There are even more rules, but don't worry too much. Just enjoy yourself—and, as we say in Korean, "*Gunbae!*" ("Cheers!").

Arts & Entertainment Best Bets

Best **Temporary Exhibitions**
★★★ Seoul Arts Center, *700 Seocho-dong, Seocho-gu (p 118)*

Best **Museum**
★★ National Museum of Korea, *135 Seobinggo-ro, Yongsan-gu (p 119)*

Best **Art Museum**
★★ Leeum, Samsung Museum of Art, *747-18 Hannam-dong, Yongsan-gu (p 119)*

Best **Live Performance**
★★★ Chongdong Nanta Theater, *15-5 Jeong-dong, Jung-gu (p 121)*

Best **Concert/Theater Venue**
★★ LG Arts Center, *679 Yeoksam 1(il)-dong, Gangnam-gu (p 123)*

Best **Amusement Complex**
★★ 63 City, *60 Yeouido-dong, Yeongdeungpo-gu (p 118)*

Best **Music Venue**
★★ Sejong Center for the Performing Arts, *81-3 Sejong-no, Jongno-gu (p 122)*

Best **Arts Complex**
★★★ Ssamziegil, *38 Gwanhun-dong, Jongno-gu (p 36)*

Best **Converted Hanok (Traditional House) Gallery**
★★★ Kyung-in Museum of Fine Art, *30-1 Gwanhun-dong, Jongno-gu (p 36)*

Exhibit at 63 SkyArt Gallery.

Jongno Arts & Entertainment

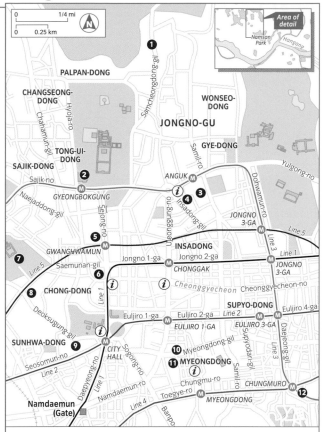

CGV Myeongdong CGV명동 **11**

Cheongdong Nanta Theater
정동난타전용관 **8**

Korea House 한국의집 **12**

Kyung-in Museum of Fine Art
경인미술관 **3**

Myeongdong Theatre
명동예술극장 **10**

National Folk Museum
국립민속박물관 **1**

National Palace Museum
국립고궁박물관 **2**

Sejong Center for the Performing Arts
세종문화회관 **5**

Seoul City Tour Bus **6**

Seoul Museum of Art
서울시립미술관 **9**

Seoul Museum of History
서울역사박물관 **7**

Ssamziegil 쌈지길 **4**

Photo p 113: Painting at the Seoul Museum of Art.

Seoul Arts & Entertainment
Best Bets

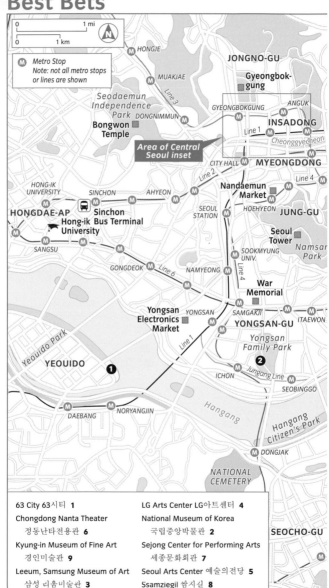

Metro Stop
Note: not all metro stops or lines are shown

HONGJE

JONGNO-GU

MUAKJAE

Gyeongbok-gung

Line 3

Seodaemun Independence Park DONGNIMMUN

GYEONGBOKGUNG

ANGUK

Bongwon Temple

INSADONG

Line 1

Cheonggyecheon

Area of Central Seoul inset

CITY HALL

MYEONGDONG

HONG-IK UNIVERSITY

SINCHON

AHYEON

Line 2

Line 4

Nandaemun Market

HONGDAE-AP

Sinchon Bus Terminal

SEOUL STATION

HOEHYEON

JUNG-GU

Hong-ik University

Seoul Tower

SANGSU

SOOKMYUNG UNIV.

Namsan Park

GONGDEOK

Line 6

NAMYEONG

Line 4

War Memorial

Yongsan Electronics Market

YONGSAN

SAMGAKJI

ITAEWON

YONGSAN-GU

Yongsan Family Park

Yeouido Park

YEOUIDO ❶

❷

ICHON

Jungang Line

SEOBINGGO

DAEBANG

NORYANGJIN

Hangang

Hangang Citizen's Park

Line 1

DONGJAK

NATIONAL CEMETERY

SEOCHO-GU

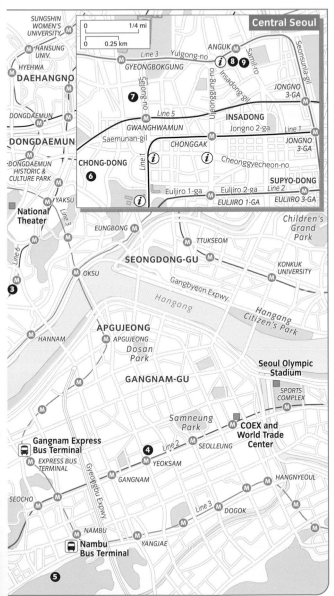

Arts & Entertainment A to Z

Amusement Complexes

★★ **kids** **63 City** YEOUIDO   This 60-story gold tower (three of its floors are underground) houses an aquarium, an IMAX theater, and a wax museum. **63 SkyArt,** a gallery showing famous international artists, is on the top floor. Dine with a view at **Walking on the Cloud** (p 98), or just pick up some pastries at **Eric Kayser** (p 92). The theater in the B1 level houses the **Fanta-Stick** Theatre (p 122). For more info, see p 25. *60 Yeouido-dong, Yeong-deungpo-gu.* ☎ *02/789-5679. Gallery, aquarium, and wax museum daily 10am–10pm, IMAX theater Tues-Sun 10am–5:30pm, Mon 10am–8:30pm. Admission prices vary by attraction. Subway: Yeouinaru, line 5 (exit 4); then take free shuttle. Map p 116.*

Arts Complexes

★★★ **Seoul Arts Center** SEO-CHO   The largest art center in the city, it houses an art museum, design gallery, opera house, concert hall, and performance theater. The Seoul National Symphony and the Korea Philharmonic perform here. Productions of world-class operas

are held here often. Changing art includes international art and photo exhibits, historic Korean art, and more. A couple of cafes, restaurants, and an ice-cream shop are on-site as well. *700 Seocho-dong, Seocho-gu.* ☎ *02/580-1300. www.sac.or.kr. Mar–Oct daily 11am–8pm; Nov–Feb daily 11am–7pm. Performance times vary. Closed every last Mon of the month. Subway: Nambu Bus Terminal, line 3 (exit 5). Map p 116.*

Dinner & a Show

★★ **Korea House** JUNG-GU   Enjoy a well-prepared royal court meal in a hanok while viewing music and dance performances. They also have traditional cultural experience programs on weekdays; check with them for times and the type of programs available. *80-2-beonji Pil-dong 2(i)-ga, Jung-gu.* ☎ *02/2266-9101. Reservations required. Grounds open daily 9am–10pm. Lunch daily noon–2pm, dinner Tues–Sat 5:30–7pm or 7:20–8:50pm, Sun 5:30–8pm. Cultural experience program Mon–Fri 9–11am or 2:30–4:30pm. www. kangkoku.or.kr. Subway: Chungmuro, line 3 or 4 (exit 3) Map p 115.*

Seoul Arts Center.

Sculpture (by Louise Bourgeois) outside the Leeum Samsung Museum of Art.

Note: Other restaurants that offer shows are listed in chapter 6, "The Best Dining."

Art Museums

★★ Leeum, Samsung Museum of Art YONGSAN   This modern building houses Buddhist art, Korean ceramics, paintings, calligraphy, and contemporary art from Korean and international artists. There are 90-minute English tours at 3pm Saturday and Sunday. *747-18 Hannam-dong, Yongsan-gu. ☎ 02/ 2014-6900. www.leeum.org. ₩10,000 adults, ₩6,000 youths. Tues–Sun 10:30am–6pm. Subway: Hangangjin, line 6 (exit 1). Bus: 11 or 0014. Map p 116.*

Seoul Museum of Art JUNG-GU SeMA exhibits both Korean and contemporary international artists inside the building of the former Korean Supreme Court. Check their exhibition schedule since galleries are closed during art installations. *37 Seosomun-dong, Jung-gu. ☎ 02/ 2124-8800. http://seoulmoa.seoul. go.kr (Korean only). ₩700 adults, ₩300 students under age 24, free ages 12 and under and 65 and over. Tues–Fri 10am–9pm; Sat–Sun 10am– 7pm (until 6pm Nov–Feb). Subway: City Hall, line 1 (exit 1) or line 2 (exit 11 or 12). Map p 115.*

National Museums

★★ National Museum of Korea YONGSAN   This giant museum exhibits Buddhist sculptures; metal works; maps; ceramics; art from Indonesia, central Asia, Japan, and China; calligraphy; paintings; and ancient relics. Free tours in English 10:30am and 2:30pm daily. *135 Seobinggo-ro, Yongsan-gu. ☎ 02/2077-9000. www.museum. go.kr. Free admission, except for tickets to certain special exhibitions. Tues, Thurs, and Fri 9am–6pm; Wed and Sat 9am–9pm; Sun and holidays 9am– 7pm; last entry 1 hr. before closing. Admission to Children's Museum free, every 90 min. 9am–4:30pm. Subway: Ichon, line 4 (exit 2). Map p 116.*

The Seoul Museum of Art.

National Museum of Korea.

Specialized Museums

Seoul has a large number of small private "museums," which are usually the personal collections of enthusiasts, specializing in everything from chickens to rice cakes. Some of them are listed in chapter 3 under the Insadong and Samcheong-dong neighborhood tours as well.

★ Lock Museum DAEHANGNO

If you're really into locks or just curious about them, this is the place for you. Historic locks and antique items from other countries are the highlights. *4F, 187-8 Dong-sung-dong, Jongno-gu.* ☎ *02/766-6494. www.lockmuseum.org. Tues–Sun 10am–6pm. Admission ₩5,000 adults, ₩3,000 ages 13–18, ₩2,000 ages 6–12, free for ages 5 and under. Subway: Hyehwa, line 4 (exit 2). Map p 120.*

Museum of Korea Straw and Plants Handicraft

MYEONGNYUN-DONG   Founded by a woman obsessed with items made of straw and who has more than 3,500 such objects in her collection. *8-4 Myeongnyun 2(i)-ga, Jongno-gu.* ☎ *02/743-8787. http://zipul.co.kr. Daily 10am–5pm (Nov–Feb), until 5:30pm (Mar–Oct), last admission 1 hr. before closing. Subway: Hyehwa, line 4 (exit 4). Bus: 101, 102, 107, 150, or 161.*

Seoul City Tour Bus

If you're short on time, take the tour bus run by the city of Seoul. Hop on the double-decker in front of the Donghwa DFS in Gwanghwamun, or any of the other 28 stops along the way. It's an efficient way to get an overview of the city. Buses leave daily every 30 minutes from 9am to 7pm, with a full tour taking 2 hours. Tour guides speak English, Japanese, and a few other languages. They also provide headsets with information available in five languages. Just look for the red, white, and blue Seoul City Tour Bus signs in front of any of the 28 locales. One-time passes cost ₩5,000 for adults, ₩3,000 for kids. A 1-day pass costs ₩10,000 for adults, ₩8,000 for children, and you can purchase tickets on the bus itself. The nighttime tour departs at 8pm and is a boring tour of the river's bridges with a stop for a bathroom break and to see the water/light show off the Danpo Bridge. For more details, check out http://en.seoulcitybus.com or call ☎ **02/777-6090.** Closed Monday.

Lock Museum.

Cinema

CGV Myeongdong MYEONG-
DONG Located on the eighth floor of
a mega shopping mall, everything
from Hollywood blockbusters to the
latest Korean fare are shown on its
five screens. The CGV theater here
and at Gangnam, Guro, and Yongsan show films with English subti-
tles. *8F, 83-5 Myeongdong 2(i)-ga,
Jung-gu. ☎ 02/1544-1122. www.cgv.
co.kr. Open daily, showtimes vary.
Subway: line 4, Myeongdong, exit 6
or line 2 to Euljiro 1(il)-ga station,
exit 6. Map p 115.*

★★ CGV Yongsan YONGSAN
South Korea's first IMAX theater also
has the country's largest screen (so
large that some say you can even
see the entire image at once). It can
seat over 2,400 people. They usually
show Korean films with English subti-
tles, as well as English-language mov-
ies. *I'Park Mall, 40-99 Hangangro
3(sam)-ga, Yongsan-gu. ☎ 02/1544-
1122. www.cgv.co.kr. Open daily,
showtimes vary. Subway: line 1,
Yongsan. From the 3F lounge area,
go toward I'Park Mall and take the
outside stairs near the event plaza.*
Or line 4 to Sinyongsan (exit 4) and
enter E-Mart and go to the 6th floor.

★ Megabox Cineplex GANG-
NAM Its 16 screens attract a
younger crowd. The European-Mega
Film Festival is held here, usually in
the late fall. *COEX Mall, 159-1 Sam-
seon-dong, Gangnam-gu. ☎ 02/
6002-1200. www.megabox.co.kr.
Open daily, showtimes vary. Subway: line 2 Samseong, exit 5 or 6.*

Nonverbal Performances

**★★★ Chongdong Nanta Thea-
ter** JUNG-GU A modernized version of Korea's folk drum tradition
called *samul nori*, this nonverbal
performance features four chefs
preparing a wedding banquet in
their musical kitchen. Other locations in Myeongdong and Gangnam.
*🕐 100 min. 15-5 Jeong-dong, Jung-
gu. ☎ 02/778-9817. http://nanta.
i-pmc.co.kr. Admission ₩40,000 and
up. Mon–Fri and Sun 5 and 8pm;
additional 2pm show Sat. Subway:
Seodaemun, line 5 (exit 5). Bus: 160,
161, 260, 270, or 271. Map p 115
and 116.*

Megabox Cineplex.

★ **Fanta-Stick** YEOUIDO   On the B1 level of the 63 City building (p 118), this 80-minute modern interpretation performance mixes samul nori with break-dancing and martial arts set to the plot of *Romeo and Juliet*. *60 Yeouido-dong, Yeong-deungpo-gu.* ☎ *02/789-5663. www. fanta-stick.co.kr. Admission ₩30,000 and up. Tues–Sun 8pm. Subway:*

Display at Sejong Center for the Performing Arts.

Yeouinaru, line 5 (exit 4); then take free shuttle.

Performance Centers
KBS Hall YEOUIDO   This small venue is home to the KBS Philhar-monic and the KBS Traditional Music orchestras. *46-beonji Yeouido-dong, Yeongdeungpo-gu.* ☎ *02/781-1000. http://office.kbs.co.kr/kbshall (Korean only). Subway: National Assembly, line 9 (exit 4) or Yeouido, line 5 (exit 3).*

★★ **National Gugak Center** SEOCHO   Modeled after the for-tress in Suwon, this government organization was created to pre-serve traditional Korean performing arts. In three indoor halls, traditional music (the Court Music Orchestra has its home here), dance, and the traditional musical drama (called *changgeuk*) are performed. They hold free performances on the out-door stage on national holidays. The on-site **Museum of Gugak ("Tradi-tional Music")** is a good place to get a bit of education, see tradi-tional instruments, and view videos of traditional performances. *700 Seocho 3(sam)-dong, Seocho-gu.* ☎ *02/580-3300. www.gugak.go.kr. Box office open Mon–Fri 9am–6pm. Tickets ₩8,000 and ₩10,000. Sub-way: Sadang, line 4 (exit 3), and then take green bus no. 17; or go to Nambu Terminal, line 3 (exit 5), and then take green bus no. 12. Bus: 142, 406, or 5413. Shuttle bus ser-vice to the subway is available after the show.*

★★ **Sejong Center for the Per-forming Arts** JONGNO   A large concert venue for traditional perfor-mances and rock concerts, it also has galleries and a small hall for chamber orchestra concerts. *81-3 Sejong-no, Jongno-gu.* ☎ *02/399-1114. www.sejongpac.or.kr. Sub-way: Gwanghwamun, line 5 (exit 1 or 8). Map p 115 and 116.*

Take Me Out to a Ball Game

Although baseball wasn't introduced to Korea until 1905 (by an American missionary), it's a popular sport throughout South Korea now. A professional league with six teams was created in 1981 with the first game in Dongdaemun Stadium on March 27, 1982 to a sold-out audience. Currently, eight teams compete in the Korean Baseball League. South Koreans love their baseball and the enthusiasm of the fans makes the games great fun. It's not difficult to go to the stadium the day of a game and get tickets, or you can get tickets in advance from ticket brokers such as **Ticketlink** (www.ticketlink.co.kr; ☎ **02/1588-7890**) or **Interpark** (www.interpark.com; ☎ **02/1588-1555**), which are Korean only unfortunately. Tickets for Jamsil Stadium games can be purchased from the teams' websites as well (see below).

Sports

★★ Jamsil Baseball Stadium

JAMSIL   Home stadium to the **LG Twins** (www.lgtwins.com) and the **Doosan Bears** (www.doosanbears.com), two out of the three teams based in Seoul. It has 30,625 seats and is part of the Jamsil Sports Complex, located near the Olympic Stadium. Games are held here during baseball season, which runs from March to October (except for when they take a break in the summer). The food selections (both inside and outside the stadium) are quite good. Games usually start at 6:30pm. *10 Jamsil 1(il)-dong, Songpa-gu.* ☎ *02/2005-0114. Tickets ₩7,000 and up. Subway: Sports Complex, line 2 (exit 5 or 6).*

★ Mokdong Baseball Stadium

YANGCHEON   This stadium is home to the **NEXEN Heroes** (www.heroes-baseball.co.kr). It has a capacity of 16,165 seats, which means it'll be a bit more intimate than a larger stadium. *914 Mokdong, Yangcheon-gu.* ☎ *02/360-1000. Tickets range from ₩5,000 to ₩15,000. Subway: Omok-gyo, line 5 (exit 2).*

★ Seoul World Cup Stadium

SEONGSAN-DONG   The largest soccer-only stadium in Asia, it is home to **FC Seoul** (www.fcseoul.com). It has over 67,000 seats and was built for the 2002 FIFA World Cup. Now, it's also a shopping complex with a 10-screen CGV Cineplex. See p 75 for info about adjacent parks. *549 Seongsan-dong, Mapo-gu.* ☎ *02/2016-2002. Stadium open daily 9am–6pm. Admission ₩1,000. Tickets to soccer games ₩8,000 and up for adults, discounts for children and teens. Subway: World Cup Stadium, line 6 (exit 1 or 2).*

Theater

★★ LG Arts Center

GANGNAM   A modern theater space designed with acoustic experiences in mind, it has three levels of seating for 1,103 people. Performances range from ballet and classical to rock concerts and musical theater, such as *Billy Elliot*. *679 Yeoksam 1(il)-dong, Gangnam-gu.* ☎ *02/2005-0114. www.lgart.com. Subway: Yeoksam, line 2 (exit 7). Map p 116.*

Myeongdong Theatre MYEONG-DONG   This was the city's premier theater from 1934 until it closed in 1975. Reopened in 2008, it features Korean interpretations of Western opera and performances such as *Cyrano de Bergerac*. *54 Myeong-dong 1(il)-ga, Jung-gu.* ☎ *02/1644-2003. www.mdtheater.or.kr. Box office Mon–Fri 10am–6pm, Sat–Sun and holidays 10am–5pm. Admission ₩20,000–₩50,000. Subway: Euljiro 1(il)-ga, line 2 (exit 6) or Myeong-dong, line 4 (exit 6). Map p 115.*

Namsan Arts Center MYEONG-DONG   Remodeled during summer 2009, it hosts stage performances of modern plays and experimental theater. Unfortunately, most of the productions are in Korean only. *8-19 Yejang-dong, Jung-gu.* ☎ *02/758-2000, or 02/1544-1555 for tickets. www.nsartscenter.or.kr. Box office Mon–Fri 9am–6pm. Subway: Myeong-dong, line 4 (exit 1).*

★ **National Theater** NAMSAN   Located on the slopes of Namsan, it is home to the national drama, dance, *changgeuk* (Korean opera),

Performance on the gayageom, *a 12-stringed zither.*

and orchestra companies. It has both small and large spaces and an outdoor stage (where they hold free concerts in the summer). *San 14-67 Jangchung-dong 2(i)-ga, Jung-gu.* ☎ *02/2280-4114. www.ntok.go.kr. Subway: Dongguk Univ., line 3 (exit 2, then the shuttle bus; or exit 6, then a 15-min. walk or take yellow bus no. 02 or 05).* ●

Take a Ferry on the Han River

The most romantic boat ride along the Hangang is the last one of the evening. There are two excursion cruises available from Yeouido: The circular line goes to Yanghwa, turns east at Dongjak Bridge, and returns to Yeouido; the other goes one-way to Ttukseom. Boats run every hour during popular summer months (July–Aug) and every 1½ to 2 hours in the spring and fall (the river freezes in the winter, making boat tours impossible). The night cruise departs around 7:30pm, though times vary, so call ahead. The trip costs ₩16,000 adults, ₩8,000 children for the live music cruise (which lasts about 80 min.); it's ₩11,000 for the quieter 50-minute cruise. They don't take reservations, so come early, especially during the popular summer months. For additional info, call ☎ **02/3271-6900.**

9 The Best **Lodging**

Lodging Best Bets

Best **Business Hotel**
★★★ Westin Chosun Hotel $$$$
87 Sogong-dong, Jung-gu (p 136)

Best **Korean-style Hotel**
★★★ The Shilla Seoul $$$$ *202 Jangchung-dong 2(i)-ga, Jung-gu (p 135)*

Best **Residence Hotel**
★★★ Somerset Palace Seoul $$$
85 Susong-dong, Jongno-gu (p 135)

Best **Mid-priced Option**
★★★ Ibis Ambassador Myeong-dong $$ *59-5 Myeongdong 1(il)-ga, Jung-gu (p 133)*

Best **Health & Fitness Facilities**
★★ COEX InterContinental Seoul $$$$ *524 Bongeunsa-ro, Gangnam-gu (p 130)*

Best **Hotel Restaurant**
★★ Sheraton Grande Walkerhill $$$$ *San 21 Gwangjang-dong, Gwangjin-gu (p 135)*

Best **Design**
★★★ Park Hyatt Seoul $$$$
995-14 Daechi 3(sam)-dong, Gangnam-gu (p 134)

Best **Value**
★★ Hill House Hotel $$ *133-1 Hoehyeon-dong 1(il)-ga, Jung-gu (p 132)*

Best **Newcomer**
★★★ IP Boutique Hotel $$ *737-32 Hannam-dong, Yongsang-gu (p 133)*

Most **Comfortable Beds**
★★ W Seoul Walkerhill $$$$
21 Gwangjang-dong, Gwangjin-gu (p 136)

Best **Family Hotel**
★★★ Fraser Suites Insadong $$$
272 Nakwon-dong, Jongno-gu (p 130)

Best **for Solo Travelers on a Budget**
★★ Stay Korea Guest House $ *66-4 Yeonnam-dong, Mapo-gu (p 136)*

Best **Hanok (Korean Traditional House)**
★★★ Rakkojae $$$$ *98 Gye-dong, Jongno-gu (p 134)*

Best **Budget Hanok (Korean Traditional House)**
★★ Tea GuestHouse $ *15-6 Gye-dong, Jongno-gu (p 136)*

The Aston House at Sheraton Grande Walkerhill.

Jongno Lodging

Beewon Guest House
비원게스트하우스 **5**

Bukchon Guest House
북촌게스트하우스 **1**

Doulos Hotel 둘로스호텔 **10**

Fraser Suites Insadong
프레이저스위츠 서울 **7**

Hotel Sunbee 호텔썬비 **9**

Koreana Hotel 코리아나호텔 **13**

Lotte Hotel 롯데호텔 **12**

Metro Hotel Myungdong
명동 메트로호텔 **11**

Rakkojae 락고재 **4**

Seoul Guest House 서울게스트하우스 **3**

Somerset Palace Seoul
서머셋팰리스서울 **6**

Tea GuestHouse 티게스트하우스 **2**

The Plaza 플라자호텔 **14**

Westin Chosun 웨스틴 조선호텔 **15**

YMCA **8**

Photo p 125: A room at The Plaza.

Seoul Lodging **Best Bets**

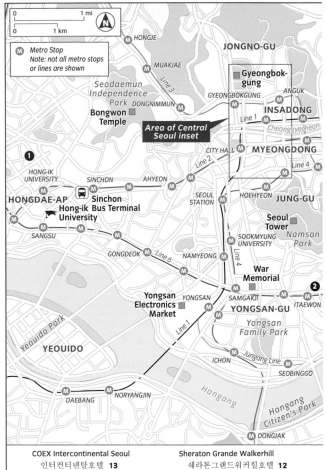

COEX Intercontinental Seoul
인터컨티넨탈호텔 **13**

Fraser Suites Insadong
프레이저스위츠 서울 **7**

Hill House Hotel 힐하우스 호텔 **9**

Ibis Ambassador Myeongdong
이비스 앰배서더 호텔 **10**

IP Boutique Hotel
아이피부티크호텔 **2**

Rakkojae 락고재 **5**

Sheraton Grande Walkerhill
쉐라톤그랜드워커힐호텔 **12**

Somerset Palace Seoul
서머셋팰리스 서울 **6**

Stay Korea Guest House
코리아 게스트 하우스 **1**

Tea GuestHouse 티게스트하우스 **4**

The Shilla Seoul 신라호텔 **3**

W Seoul Walkerhill W워커힐 호텔 **11**

Westin Chosun Hotel
웨스틴 조선호텔 **8**

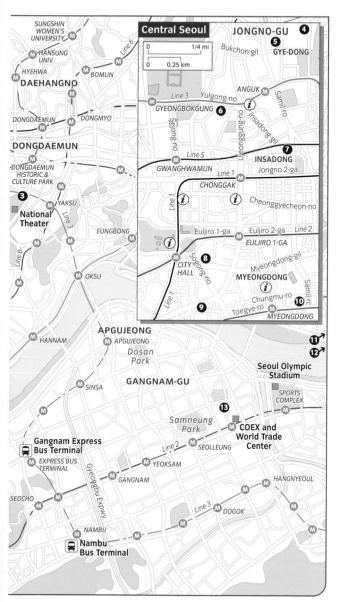

Seoul Hotels A to Z

★ Beewon Guest House INSA-DONG Great for budget travelers, it has double and dorm-style rooms. It also has shared bathrooms and a kitchen, as well as lockers and laundry. *28-2 Unni-dong, Jongno-gu.* ☎ *02/765-0670. www.beewonguesthouse.com. 8 units. ₩19,000/bed; ₩50,000 double. Rates include continental breakfast. MC, V. Map p 127.*

★ Best Western Premier Kukdo JUNG-GU A dependable choice, especially given the price and location, this tourist-class hotel has most modern amenities. However, Internet access is available only in the lobby. *310 Euljiro 4 (sa)-ga, Jung-gu.* ☎ *02/6466-1234. www.bestwestern.com. 295 units. ₩100,000 and up. AE, DC, MC, V.*

★★ Bukchon Guest House BUK-CHON Although it's a converted hanok, you can choose between *ondol*-style rooms (Korean-style rooms with floor mats) or those with beds. Shared baths. **Note:** Book well in advance, since the units tend to fill up fast. *72 Gye-dong, Jongno-gu.* ☎ *02/743-8530. www.bukchon72.com. 5 units. ₩35,000 and up. AE, MC, V. Map p 127.*

★★ COEX InterContinental Seoul GANGNAM Connected to the COEX complex, this hotel is great for those attending a convention at the COEX or conducting business in the area. *524 Bongeunsa-ro, Gangnam-gu.* ☎ *02/3452-2500. www.ichotelsgroup.com. 652 units. ₩230,000 and up. Additional 11% VAT. AE, DC, MC, V. Map p 128.*

★★ Co-op Residence (Sinchon Central) SINCHON Staying here is like renting your own apartment, with spacious units that have modern bathrooms; all feature kitchens

and dining areas. Staff are responsive to your needs. Other locations near Dongdaemun, Yeouido, and Euljiro. *57-26 Nogosan-dong, Mapo-gu.* ☎ *02/6220-4000. http://rent.co-op.co.kr. 183 units. ₩140,000 and up. AE, DC, MC, V.*

★★ Doulos Hotel INSADONG Although the rooms are a bit small, they have hardwood floors and clean-line furnishings at this hotel, hidden down a small alley. English-speaking staff go out of their way to be helpful. Coin laundry is available. *112 Gwansu-dong, Jung-gu.* ☎ *02/2266-2244. http://douloshotel.com. 44 units. ₩100,000 and up w/breakfast. Additional 10% VAT. MC, V. Map p 127.*

★★★ kids Fraser Suites Insadong INSADONG This all-suite hotel is in the *yangban* neighborhood, where the old aristocrats once lived. Fantastic for families, all have kitchens, living rooms, dining rooms, and a study area. There are no dishwashers, but housekeeping does the dirty dishes. The kids will love the playroom and free DVD rentals. *272 Nakwon-dong, Jongno-gu.* ☎ *02/6262-8282. http://seoul.frasershospitality.com. 213 units. ₩200,000 and up. AE, MC, V. Map p 127 and 128.*

★★★ Grand Ambassador Seoul JONGNO Close to Namdaemun and Itaewon, it has newly renovated rooms that are elegant and up-to-date. It's quite a value for the location. *186-54 Jangchung-dong 2(i)-ga, Jung-gu.* ☎ *02/2275-1101. www.accorhotels.com. 409 units. ₩131,000 and up. AE, DC, MC, V.*

★★ Grand Hyatt NAMSAN Be sure to ask for a city view when you check in here. Beds are hard, and bathrooms are small but make use

Lobby at the Grand Ambassador Seoul.

of the limited space. Fitness facilities and sauna are modern but come at a premium. *747-7 Hannam 2(i)-dong, Yongsan-gu.* ☎ *02/797-1234. http:// seoul.grand.hyatt.com. 601 units. ₩256,000 and up w/breakfast. Additional 10% VAT and 10% service charge. AE, DC, MC, V.*

★★★ Grand InterContinental Seoul GANGNAM
A top-notch hotel next to CALT limousine bus and the COEX convention center, its lobby, rooms, and facilities are spacious and contemporary without feeling impersonal. *521 Teheran-no, Gangnam-gu.* ☎ *02/555-5656. www. ichotelsgroup.com. 510 units. ₩191,300 and up. Additional 11% VAT. AE, DC, MC, V.*

Hamilton Hotel ITAEWON The best thing going for this old standard is its strategic location (and it's actually a landmark in the area). The rooms are a bit dated but relatively

Homestay in a Folk House

The Korean traditional home, the hanok, used to be the norm until the 1970s, when post-war development focused on modernizing everything (yielding to the multistoried concrete apartment complexes of today). The opening up of the Bukchon Hanok Maeul has inspired some of its residents to open their doors for guest stays. These converted hanok have been upgraded with modern amenities (flushing toilets, satellite TV, and Internet service). Most only have a few rooms, so book early during the popular summer months. Most of them are located on the lower outskirts of the Bukchon folk village. Costs are a reasonable ₩35,000 and up, but the experience is priceless.

We recommend a stay at **Bukchon Guest House** (see previous page), **Seoul Guest House** (p 134), or the **Tea GuestHouse** (p 136). If you're lucky enough to snag the only room at **Sosunjae** (☎ **011/9853-6627;** thinkmuse@naver.com), you'll be treated to a delicious Korean breakfast daily and see the occasional schoolchildren, who visit the hanok "museum" to see traditional culture and history. Prices are ₩100,000 for single occupancy, ₩130,000 double.

Lobby at the Grand InterContinental Seoul.

☎ 02/771-8135. 30 units. ₩83,000 and up. MC, V. Map p 128.

★★ Hotel Prince Seoul

MYEONGDONG A good value for the location and modern amenities; even noise isn't much of a problem. English-speaking staff are very helpful. *1-1 Namsan-dong 2(i)-ga, Jung-gu.* ☎ *02/752-7111. www. hotelprinceseoul.co.kr. 87 units. ₩130,000 and up. Additional 10% VAT. AE, DC, MC, V.*

Hotel Seokyo HONGDAE-AP

A standard business hotel with no frills, and its facilities show some wear and tear. But it's one of the few hotels in the area and useful for easy access to the airport. *354-5 Seogyo-dong, Mapo-gu.* ☎ *02/330-7777. www.hotelseokyo.co.kr. 115 units. ₩200,000 and up. AE, MC, V.*

★★★ Hotel the Sunbee INSA-

DONG One of the best mid-priced options, its rooms come with hardwood floors and marble bathrooms. Many have computers and free Internet access, so ask for one at check-in. *198-11 Gwanhun-dong, Jung-gu.* ☎ *02/730-3451. www. hotelsunbee.com. 42 units. ₩77,000 and up. MC, V. Map p 127.*

spacious. The beds are almost militaristic in their firmness. *119-25 Itae-won-dong, Yongsan-gu.* ☎ *02/6393-1234. www.hamilton.co.kr. 166 units. ₩90,000 and up. Additional 10% VAT and 10% service charge. AE, DC, MC, V.*

★★ Hill House Hotel MYEONG-

DONG Conveniently located (although it's a bit of an uphill walk from the subway station), this hotel is a solid, mid-priced option. Rooms are spacious and comfortable, and the free breakfast is a plus, especially for the price. *133-1 Hoehyeon-dong 1(il)-ga, Jung-gu.*

Choosing a Seoul Hotel

Given Seoul's sprawling layout and the number of hotels, deciding where to stay may seem like a difficult decision. Luckily, most hotels are walking distance to a subway station, and taxis are easily flagged down on any street. Luxury lovers opt for the high-end hotels in Gangnam, while business travelers gravitate toward the financial district and Jongno. If you want to be in the middle of the tourist district, Insadong or Myeongdong are good neighborhoods from which to choose. For a more international flair, Itaewon is your best bet. Convenient to clubs and universities are the areas near Sinchon, Idea-ap, and Hongdae-ap. Those wanting a retreat away from the city prefer the quieter digs on Namsan, Walkerhill, or Gwangjin, though you'll have to take a taxi into the city.

★★★ Ibis Seoul Myeongdong

MYEONGDONG   An exceptional value for the price and location, it has simple decor, firm beds, and good water pressure. The free Internet and on-site bathhouse are great perks. *59-5 Myeongdong 1(il)-ga, Jung-gu.* ☎ *02/6361-8888. www. accorhotels.com. 280 units. ₩105,000 and up. AE, DC, MC, V. Map p 128.*

★ Imperial Palace

GANGNAM   A luxury business hotel convenient to the COEX convention center, it may have a dark-wood, stuffy decor, but it also has excellent service and comfortable rooms. *248-7 Nonhyeon-dong, Gangnam-gu.* ☎ *02/3440-8000. www.imperialpalace.co.kr. 430 units. ₩300,000 and up. Additional 10% VAT and 10% service charge. AE, MC, V.*

★★★ IP Boutique Hotel

ITAEWON   This modernist hotel comes with HDTVs, free Wi-Fi, and iPod docking stations. Pop art, glass, and mirrors make this a fun stay for those looking for something different. *737-32 Hannam-dong, Yongsan-gu.* ☎ *02/3702-8000. www.ipboutique hotel.com. 131 units. ₩200,000 double; ₩375,000 suite. MC, V. Map p 128.*

★★ JW Marriott

GANGNAM   A 35-story contemporary hotel, it connects to the COEX Mall and caters to business travelers. Beds have down comforters, and bathrooms are high-tech. *19-3 Banpo-dong, Seocho-gu.* ☎ *02/6282-6262. www.marriott. com. 497 units. ₩225,000 and up. Additional 10% VAT and 10% service charge. AE, DC, MC, V.*

Kim's Guest House

SINCHON   This cozy little guesthouse has dorm-style beds and private rooms. Not fancy digs, but the friendly owner makes you feel like family. *443-16 Hapjeong-dong, Mapo-gu.* ☎ *02/337-9894. www.kimsguest house.com. 12 units. ₩18,000/bed; ₩35,000 single. MC, V (extra 4% for credit card payments).*

★ Koreana Hotel

JONGNO   A pleasant hotel with a pleasant staff, the 14-story building is centrally located to explore the city. Rooms are spacious enough, but the desk is tiny. *61-1 Taepyeong-no 1(il)-ga, Jung-gu.* ☎ *02/2171-7000. www. koreanahotel.com. 344 units. ₩215,000 and up. AE, DC, MC, V. Map p 127.*

★★ Lotte Hotel

JONGNO   One of the city's largest hotels, its newer second tower is connected by a tri-level mall. A world-class hotel, it's convenient to the financial district. *1, Sogong-dong, Jung-gu.* ☎ *02/ 771-1000. www.lottehotel.co.kr. 478 units. ₩290,000 and up. Additional 10% VAT and 10% service charge. AE, DC, MC, V. Map p 127.*

★★★ Metro Hotel Myungdong

MYEONGDONG   The rooms are comfortable and a decent size at this well-priced hotel with free breakfast and Internet access. *99-33 Euljiro 2(i)-ga, Jung-gu.* ☎ *02/757-1112. http://metrohotel.co.kr. 75 units. ₩80,000 and up. Additional 10% VAT. AE, MC, V. Map p 127.*

A stylish suite at IP Boutique Hotel.

A suite at the Park Hyatt.

Myeong Dong Guest House
MYEONGDONG   Though rooms are
pretty basic, this guesthouse is conveniently located and affordable.
The bathrooms are tiny, but facilities are well kept by an amicable
middle-aged couple. *17 Namsan-
dong 3(sam)-ga, Jung-gu.* ☎ *02/755-
5437. www.mdguesthouse.com. 45
units. ₩30,000 and up. MC, V.*

★★ Millennium Seoul Hilton
NAMSAN   Within walking distance
to Namdaemun Market, it's located
at the foot of Namsan. Although the
building is a bit dated, the rooms
are still comfortable. *395 Namdae-
mun-no 5(o)-ga, Jung-gu.* ☎ *02/317-
3114. www.hilton.com. 683 units.
₩220,000 and up. Additional 10%
VAT and 10% service charge. AE, DC,
MC, V.*

★★★ Park Hyatt Seoul GANG-
NAM   Elegant, modern, and well-
designed, the 24-story hotel has
comfortable beds and great bathrooms. For quiet, request a room
away from the main drag. *995-14
Daechi 3(sam)-dong, Gangnam-gu.*
☎ *02/2016-1234. http://seoul.park.
hyatt.com. 185 units. ₩274,000 and
up. Additional 11% VAT and 10% service charge. AE, DC, MC, V.*

★★ The Plaza JONGNO   With a
face-lift and a new name, the former
Seoul Plaza Hotel has reinvented
itself as a boutique business hotel.
23 Taepyeong-no 2(i)-ga, Jung-gu.
☎ *02/771-2200. www.hoteltheplaza.
com. 478 units. ₩180,000 and up.
Additional 10% VAT and 10% service
charge. AE, DC, MC, V. Map p 127.*

★★★ Rakkojae BUKCHON   They
call themselves a "boutique" hanok
and the guest rooms are pretty fancy
(complete with jade floors in the
master bedroom). This 130-year-old
hanok was renovated by a master
carpenter in 2003 and offers multicourse dinners, yellow-mud saunas,
and traditional performances (for
additional fees, of course). *98 Gye-
dong, Jongno-gu.* ☎ *010/8555-1407.
www.rkj.co.kr. 4 units. ₩180,000 and
up. Cash only. Map p 127 and 128.*

★★ Seoul Guest House BUK-
CHON   The first converted hanok
to open its rooms for visitors, all
units have air-conditioning, refrigerators, and Internet access. All
rooms, except the "family" room,
have a shared bath. *135-1 Gye-dong,
Jongno-gu.* ☎ *02/745-0057. www.
seoul110.com. ₩35,000 and up. AE,
MC, V. Map p 127.*

Seoul YMCA JONGNO   You can't
get any more basic than these rooms
with hard beds, but it's a real value for
the central location. *9 Jongno 2(i)-ga,
Jongno-gu.* ☎ *02/734-6884. www.
ymca.or.kr/hotel. 30 units. ₩55,000
and up. Additional 10% VAT. AE, MC,
V. Map p 127.*

Sleeping on a Budget

Seoul has its share of luxury hotels, but inexpensive sleeping quarters are also easy to come by. Love motels are a good option for couples traveling together. They are all very similar (double bed, TV, minifridge, some with computers and Internet access) and cost anywhere from ₩30,000 to ₩45,000 per night. None of them take reservations, but it's not difficult to find a room just walking off the street (except during the popular summer months). There are plenty of guesthouses and hostels in Seoul, too, tucked down small alleyways in the major neighborhoods of the city. However, the least expensive sleeping options are the huge communal sleeping rooms (segregated by gender) in Korean bathhouses (*jjimjilbang*). Not for light sleepers, ₩8,000 to ₩10,000 will get you a soak in a bath, access to the sauna, and a super-cheap place to sleep, even if it means a hard floor and strangers snoring next to you.

★★ **Sheraton Grande Walkerhill** GWANGJIN Nestled in the hills, this hotel is great for those wanting to get away from it all. No direct subway access, but there are free shuttles. *175 Achaseong-gil, Gwangjin-gu.* ☎ *02/455-5000. www.sheratonwalkerhill.co.kr. 597 units. ₩224,000 and up. Additional 10% VAT and 10% service charge. AE, DC, MC, V. Map p 128.*

★★★ **The Shilla Seoul** NAMSAN This 16-story hotel has a minimalist lobby, but its rooms are stodgier, with stately wood furniture and

overstuffed Korean blankets. The location is a bit inconvenient, but it's great for those wanting quiet. *202 Jangchung-dong 2(i)-ga, Jung-gu.* ☎ *02/2233-3131. www.shilla.net. 507 units. ₩340,000 and up. Additional 10% VAT and 10% service charge. AE, DC, MC, V.*

★★★ **Somerset Palace Seoul** JONGNO This well-located residence hotel has all the amenities of an apartment—complete with washer and dryer, kitchen, and dining area. A 7-night minimum stay is required. *85 Susong-dong, Jongno-gu.*

Seoul Guest House.

The Shilla Seoul.

☎ 02/6730-8888. www.somerset.
com. 465 units. ₩252,000 and up.
Additional 10% VAT. AE, DC, MC, V.
Map p 127 and 128.

★★ Stay Korea Guest House
HONDAE-AP   The friendly owners
here speak English, Japanese, and
even French. A deal for solo travelers, it offers breakfast and use of the
washing machine. 66-4 Yeonnam-
dong, Mapo-gu. ☎ 02/339-9026.
www.staykorea.co.kr. 6 units.
₩19,000/bed; ₩35,000 single;
₩50,000 double. No credit cards.
Map p 128.

★★ Tea GuestHouse JONGNO
Reserve early for one of only four
quarters in this hanok run by a
friendly couple. Although the feeling
is old folk village, the facilities
have been upgraded to include air-
conditioning and Internet access.

15-6 Gye-dong, Jongno-gu. ☎ 02/
3675-9877. www.teaguesthouse.com.
4 units. ₩40,000 and up. AE, MC, V.
Map p 127 and 128.

★★★ Vabien Suites II JONGNO
Choose from studios to two bed-
rooms at this all-suite hotel. Spacious
with hardwood floors, bathrooms
have showers only, but fixtures are
modern. The in-room washer/dryers
and kitchen are a plus. 25-10 Euljiro
1(il)-ga, Jung-gu. ☎ 02/6399-0113.
286 units. ₩180,000 and up. AE, DC,
MC, V.

★★★ Westin Chosun Hotel
JONGNO   This classic was built in
1914, but it has been renovated
since. Conveniently located, high-
tech rooms have antiallergenic
carpets or wood floors. 87 Sogong-
dong, Jung-gu. ☎ 02/771-0500.
www.starwoodhotels.com. 465 units.
₩300,000 and up. Additional 11%
VAT and 10% service charge. AE, DC,
MC, V. Map p 127 and 128.

★★ W Seoul Walkerhill
GWANGJIN   Located in Achasan,
the W is great for those who want
to get away from it all but still be
near the city. The "Wonderful"
rooms have round beds, round
chairs, and even a round bathtub.
175 Achaseong-gil, Gwangjin-gu.
☎ 02/465-2222. www.starwood
hotels.com. 253 units. ₩210,000
and up. Additional 11% VAT and 10%
service charge. AE, DC, MC, V. Pets
welcome. Map p 128. ●

The pool at the Westin Chosun Hotel.

The DMZ

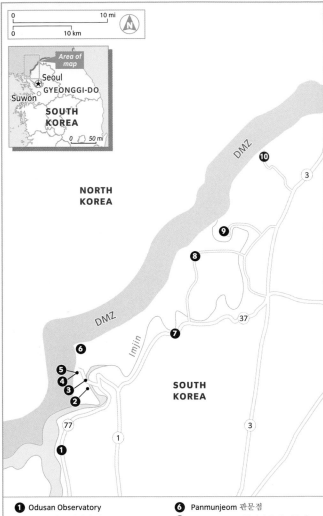

1. **Odusan Observatory**
   오두산 통일전망대
2. **Imjingak Park** 임진각 평화누리 공원
3. **Dorasan Station** 도라산역
4. **Dora Observatory** 도라전망대
5. **3rd Infiltration Tunnel** 제3땅굴

6. **Panmunjeom** 판문점
7. **Dujinaru Ferry** 두지나루 황포돛배
8. **Sangseung Observation Post**
   상승전망대
9. **Taepung Observatory** 태풍전망대
10. **Yeolsoe Observatory** 열쇠 전망대

Previous page: Manisan.

Korea's Demilitarized Zone is one of the last remnants of the Cold War. North and South Korea remains the only divided country in the world after the Korean War (1950–53). Although a peace treaty was never signed, a ceasefire ended the fighting on July 27, 1953, and created the DMZ, stretching 2km (1¼ miles) on either side of the border between the two countries on the divided peninsula.

Panmunjeom.

❶ ★★ Panmunjeom. This Joint Security Area is best known for the peace talks that ended the fighting of the Korean War on October 25, 1951. It's the only place in the DMZ where representatives from the two Koreas can meet and discuss efforts toward peace. All visitors are required to attend a 30-minute briefing at Camp Bonifas before visiting. The Bridge of No Return straddles the DMZ near the Panmunjeom.

The DMZ Practical Matters

Due to security reasons, individual visitors are not allowed into the Panmunjeom and certain areas of the DMZ without complicated advanced reservations, so we recommend taking an organized tour from Seoul, most of which cost ₩80,000 or so. Itineraries will differ by company, but most include one of the infiltration tunnels, a military base, a view from an observatory, and Panmunjeom. A list of tour options is included at the end of this section. Only areas in Paju and Yeoncheon can be visited on a day trip; areas farther east will require a rental car and at least an overnight stay.

The Bridge of No Return.

🕐 *90 min. Eoryong-ri, Jinseo-myeon, Paju-si, Gyeonggi-do. Free admission. Mon–Sat 9am–2:30pm.*

❷ ★★★ Imjingak Park. Built in 1971 in hopes of a possible reunification, the area includes several memorials, the Bridge of Freedom, tanks and other relics from the war, and a photo display of life in North Korea. It's one of the few areas in the DMZ that doesn't require a security check. 🕐 *2 hr. 1325-1 Majeong-ri, Munsan-eup, Paju-si, Gyeonggi-do. ☎ 031/953-4744. www.paju.go.kr. Admission ₩8,700 on foot, ₩11,700 monorail. Daily 10am–6pm.*

❸ ★ Odusan Unification Observatory. From its vantage point on a clear day, visitors can see both Seoul's 63 building and North

Korea's Songaksan. It also displays and sell products made in North Korea. 🕐 *90 min. 659 Seongdong-ri, Tanhyeon-myeon, Paju-si, Gyeonggi-do. ☎ 031/945-3171. www.jmd.co.kr. Admission ₩3,000 adults, ₩1,600 ages 7–18. Apr–Sept 9am–5:30pm; Nov–Feb 9am–4:30pm; Mar and Oct 9am–5pm.*

❹ ★ Dorasan Observatory & the Third Infiltration Tunnel. Discovered in 1978, this is the third of several tunnels dug by North Korean soldiers to sneak into the

The Third Infiltration Tunnel.

A Natural Habitat

The DMZ encompasses an area along 248 km (154 miles) long on land and 200km (124 miles) long in the Yellow Sea. Taking up 0.5% of the total land mass of the Korean peninsula, it is also called the Peace and Life Zone (PLZ) for the unexpected natural habitat it has spawned. The area encompasses six rivers, two mountain ranges, and a plain. Untouched by humans for more than 60 years, a third of Korea's plant species, a fifth of the bird species, and half of the different mammals that exist on the peninsula have been discovered here.

DMZ Tour Companies

All tour companies require a reservation at least 3 days in advance and only run on select days when they have enough people. Remember to bring your passport and dress conservatively.

DMZ Tour Includes a tour of the DMZ fence, Yeolsoe Observatory, Imjingak, and the Bridge of Freedom. *404 Gongdeok-dong (Poonglim Bldg. no. 506), Mapo-gu.* ☎ *02/706-4851. www.dmztourkorea.com. Admission ₩80,000 (includes lunch). Tours 8am–4pm.*

Freedom Travel Inbound Includes a tour of Imjingak, the Bridge of Freedom, the Third Infiltration Tunnel, Dora Observatory, and Dorasan Station, and stops at a ginseng center or amethyst factory. *6F, 88 Da-dong (Dong-A Bldg.), Jung-gu.* ☎ *02/772-5856. www.freedom tour.co.kr. Admission ₩46,000 regular tour, ₩65,000 with lunch. Tours daily 8am–2pm or 8am–4:30pm (includes lunch).*

International Cultural Service Club Includes a tour of Panmunjeom, the Third Infiltration Tunnel, and the DMZ fence. *6F, 1 Sogong-dong (Lotte Hotel), Jung-gu.* ☎ *02/755-0073. www.tourdmz.com. Admission ₩77,000 (includes lunch; an extra ₩1,000 on Sat). Tours Tues–Sat 8am–1:50pm or 10am–4:40pm.*

USO Tour Includes a tour of Panmunjeom, the Third Infiltration Tunnel, Dora Observatory, and Dorasan Station. *104 Galwol-dong (USP 140 [Camp Kim]), Yongsan-gu.* ☎ *02/795-3028. www.koridoor.co.kr. Admission ₩77,000, ₩39,000 for U.S. military (includes lunch). Tours 7:30am–3:30pm.*

south. The Dorasan Observatory, where a North Korean military base and Geumgangsan ("Diamond Mountains") are visible, is located nearby. From there you can catch a glimpse of a statue of Kim Il-sung on the other side. 🕐 *1 hr. Jeomwon-ri, Gunnae-myeon, Paju-si, Gyeonggi-do.* ☎ *031/940-8345. Admission monorail ₩8,700 adults, ₩8,200 ages 18 and under, ₩7,000 65 and up; on foot ₩8,200 adults, ₩6,200 youths, ₩5,500 seniors. Tues–Sun 1st ride 9:10am, last ride 3pm. Closed Mon.*

❺ ★★★ **Dujinaru Ferry.** Before the war, boats used to float along the Imjin River delivering necessities to those farther inland. Recently, sailboat rides have resumed at least along this tiny part of the Imjingang, though it doesn't run in the winter when the river freezes. 🕐 *45 min. Paju-si, Gyeonggi-do.* ☎ *031/958-2557. Admission ₩8,000 adults, ₩6,000 children. Daily 10am–6pm, closed when the river freezes in winter.*

❺ ★ **Yeolsoe Observatory.** This building was built not only as a means of viewing North Korea, but also as a way to comfort Northerners who cannot go home. Inside there is a display of everyday items from the Communist state. 🕐 *1 hr. Deoksan-ri, Sinseo-myeon, Yeoncheon-gun, Gyeonggi-do. Free admission. Daily 8am–5pm.*

Suwon

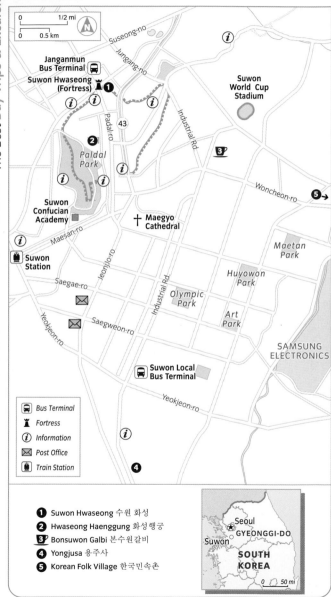

0   1/2 mi
0   0.5 km

Suseong-no
Jungang-no

Janganmun Bus Terminal
Suwon Hwaseong (Fortress) ❶

ⓘ ⓘ

Suseong-no

Suwon World Cup Stadium

Padal-ro

43

❷

Paldal Park

ⓘ

ⓘ

Industrial Rd.

Bonsuwon Galbi ❸

Woncheon-ro

❺→

Suwon Confucian Academy

Maesan-ro

✝ **Maegyo Cathedral**

Maetan Park

Jeonjo-ro

Industrial Rd.

ⓘ

Suwon Station

Saegae-ro

Huyowon Park

Olympic Park

Art Park

SAMSUNG ELECTRONICS

Yeokjeon-ro

Saegweon-ro

Suwon Local Bus Terminal

Yeokjeon-ro

ⓘ

❹

ⓘ **Bus Terminal**
♜ **Fortress**
ⓘ **Information**
✉ **Post Office**
🚉 **Train Station**

❶ Suwon Hwaseong 수원 화성
❷ Hwaseong Haenggung 화성행궁
❸ Bonsuwon Galbi 본수원갈비
❹ Yongjusa 용주사
❺ Korean Folk Village 한국민속촌

Seoul
GYEONGGI-DO
Suwon
SOUTH KOREA

0   50 mi

The capital of Gyeonggi-do is best known for the Suwon Hwaseong, the stone fortress built here by King Jeongjo in 1796 to guard his father's tomb. Only 30km (19 miles) from Seoul, the city is also known for its *galbi* (short ribs) and for its soccer stadium. Don't miss the Korean Folk Village and, for those with kids, South Korea's largest amusement park, Everland.

❶ ★★★ Suwon Hwaseong.
Finished in 1796, this UNESCO World Heritage site was restored in 1979. The impressive stone fortress used to encircle the entire city, but the city now surrounds the stone wall. If you don't want to walk the entire length of the wall, a "dragon" train on wheels is also available.
🕓 *2–3 hr. to walk the entire wall. Ingye-dong, Suwon-si, Gyeonggi-do. http://ehs.suwon.ne.kr. Admission fortress ₩1,000; dragon train ₩1,500 adults, ₩1,100 teens, ₩1,000 seniors 65 and over, ₩700 children. Open daily 24 hr. Bus: 2, 7,* *7-2, 8, or 13 across from Suwon Station (get off at Jongno 4-geoli [4-way] and walk 5 min.); or 1007 or 3000 to Jongno Station.*

❷ ★ Hwaseong Haenggung.
Built during the Joseon Dynasty, King Jeongjo stayed at this temporary palace to rest from battle during his "long journey." In good weather April to October, the guarding ceremony is held at the front gate Sundays at 2pm. On Saturdays you can see traditional performances; weekdays, the 24 Martial Arts Preservation Association

Suwon Hwaseong.

performs traditional martial arts at 11am. *Namchang-dong, Paldal-gu, Suwon-si, Gyeonggi-do. http://ehs. suwon.ne.kr. Admission ₩1,000 adults, ₩700 youths, ₩500 children, free for seniors and kids 5 and under. Mar–Oct Tues–Sun 9am–6pm; Nov–Feb Tues–Sun 10am–5pm.*

3 ★★ **Bonsuwon Galbi.** If you worked up an appetite after walking the length of the fortress, head down to this popular joint for some galbi. It has the typical tabletop grills for DIY cooking, but it also serves *galbi jjim* (stewed beef ribs) and other beef dishes. *51-20 Uman-dong, Paldal-gu, Suwon-si. ☎ 031/ 211-8434. $$$.*

4 ★ **Yongjusa.** Built during the Silla Dynasty, the original temple was destroyed during the second Manchu invasion. After a dragon dream (hence the name), King Jeongjo had a new temple built here in 1790 to honor his father. The highlights here are the dragon motifs, a massive bronze bell cast in 854, and a mural of a tiger smoking a pipe. A short walk leads to the royal tombs. *188 Song-san-ri, Taean-eup, Hwaseong-si,*

Gyeonggi-do. ☎ 031/234-9391. www.yongjoosa.or.kr (Korean only). Admission ₩1,500 adults, ₩1,000 teens, ₩700 kids. Bus: 24, 46, or 46-1 from Suwon Station.

5 ★★★ **kids** **Korean Folk Village.** More like an open-air folk museum, there are more than 260 traditional houses and buildings from the late Joseon period. Vendors in traditional costumes sell everything from strips of paper with *hanja* (traditional Chinese characters) to small sacks of pumpkin taffy. A "food court" serves traditional Korean fare at the far end of the village. Try to time your visit for a performance, which are more frequent on weekends and holidays. ⏱ *1–2 hr. 107 Bora-dong, Giheung-gu, Yon-gin-si, Gyeonggi-do. ☎ 031/288-0000. Admission ₩12,000 adults, ₩9,000 youths, ₩8,000 children; unlimited ticket ₩16,000 adults, ₩14,000 youths, ₩13,000 children. Summer daily 9am–6:30pm; winter daily 9am–5pm; opens 30 min. later Sun and holidays. Free hourly shuttle bus from Suwon Station Mon–Fri 10:30am–2:20pm and Sat–Sun 10am–2:20pm.*

6 **kids** ★★ **Everland.** The country's largest amusement park, it has

Suwon Practical Matters

Suwon is easy to get to via Seoul's subway line 1. It takes just under an hour, but it's a scenic and inexpensive ride. If you're looking for more speed, the KTX train stops in Suwon from Seoul Station (on the way to Busan) for ₩9,000. Express buses are also available from Sadang Station (no. 7770), Gangnam Station (no. 3000), or Guro Station (no. 900).

There are direct airport limousine buses from Incheon Airport (in front of gate 7A, or bus stop 3 or 12). It costs around ₩15,000 and takes about 90 minutes.

Sleeping in Suwon

Most people visit Suwon on a day trip from Seoul. However, an overnight stay would be necessary if you're visiting Everland or want to explore the area a bit further. Since the city is the capital of Gyeonggi-do, there are several affordable choices for hotels and motels. The **Ibis Ambassador Suwon** (☎ **031/230-5000;** www. ibishotel.com) has spacious rooms and modern amenities. The **Ramada Plaza Suwon** (☎ **031/230-0001;** www.ramada.com) is also well located and good for business travelers. The **Hotel Castle** (☎ **031/211-6666;** www.hcastle.co.kr), which is more Korean in style, has friendly staff. Inexpensive love motels can be found around the train station and other parts of the city.

40 rides, gardens, and a chance to see tigers, lions, giraffes, and elephants up close via the "Safari Bus Tour." **Caribbean Bay,** the water park, requires a separate admission. Though it's not in Suwon proper, it's close by. *310 Jeondae-ri, Pogok-eup, Cheoin-gu, Yongin-si, Gyeonggi-go.*

☎ 031/320-5000. www.everland. com. Admission ₩37,000 adults, ₩31,000 teens, ₩26,000 children. Daily 9:30am–10pm. Bus: 66 or 6000 from Suwon Station, or 5002 from Gangnam Station (subway line 2, exit 6).

Detail at Suwon Hwaseong.

Ganghwa-do

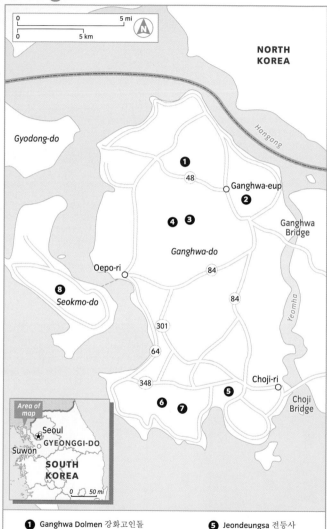

1. Ganghwa Dolmen 강화고인돌
2. Ganghwa Anglican Church
   강화 성공회성당
3. Gocheon-ri Dolmen 고천리고인돌
4. Jeokseoksa 적석사
5. Jeondeungsa 전등사
6. Manisan 마니산
7. Jeongsusa 정수사
8. Bomunsa 보문사

South Korea's coast is dotted with hundreds of islands, and Ganghwa is a one of the larger ones worth exploring. Considered part of Incheon city, it's actually a group of islands, and the main island is accessible via two bridges from the mainland. The biggest attractions are the *goindol* (dolmen) from the Bronze Age. More than 100 of them are found here (though only 70 are registered with UNESCO). They're not grouped together, so the best way to see them is to rent a car, or take a bus to the island and hire a taxi.

Ganghwa Dolmen.

❶ **Ganghwa Dolmen.** The largest table dolmen on the island, it may not seem big (the capstone is 6.4m/21 ft. long), but it's still the largest one in the country. It sits in an isolated field surrounded by a small park. *317 Bugeun-ri, Hajeom-myeon, Ganghwa-gun, Incheon-si. Free admission. Open daily 24 hr.*

❷ **★★ Ganghwa Anglican Church.** On a small hill overlooking Ganghwa Town, this church was built by a royal architect who helped reconstruct Gyeongbokgung (p 7). It is a wonderful melding of Korean palace architecture with a Roman Basilica interior. It's best to visit on Sunday morning when the interior is accessible. *Bugeun-ri, Hajeom-myeon, Ganghwa-gun, Incheon-si. Free admission. Open daily 24 hr.*

❸ **Gocheon-ri Dolmen.** Said to have been the earliest ones on the island, their location on the slopes of a mountain make them unusual. *Gocheon-ri, Naega-myeon, Ganghwa-gun, Incheon-si. Free admission.*

❹ **★ Jeokseoksa.** This small temple is perched on the western slopes of Goryeosan. The best time to visit is during sunset, for the view and the ringing of the bell. *Naega-myeon, Ganghwa-gun, Incheon-si. ☎ 032/932-6191.*

❺ **★★ Jeondeungsa.** Built in 381, the most notable parts of the temple are the carved figures of a naked woman holding up the roof of the main hall. Apparently, it depicts a barmaid who broke the heart of the temple architect and ran off with his money. Now she's destined to hold up the temple's roof for eternity.

Jeondeungsa.

Nearby is the **Onsuri Anglican Church,** one of many *hanok* (Korean traditional houses) churches found on the island (*church: free admission. Mon–Sat 9am–2:30pm).* 🕐 *90 min. 635 Onsu-ri, Gilsang-myeon, Ganghwa-gun, Incheon-si. Admission*

₩2,500 adults, ₩1,700 teens, ₩1,000 children. Daily 8am–6pm.

6 ★★ **Manisan.** The highest mountain on the island is also the best for hiking. There are two well-marked trails: The "Yangban Trail" is a gradual, gentle hike, and the "Stairway Path" makes for a steeper climb. *Hwado-myeon, Ganghwa-gun, Incheon-si.* ☎ *032/930-3114. Admission ₩1,500 adults, ₩800 teens, ₩500 children. Open daily sunrise to sunset. Bus: Direct from Sinchon Intercity Bus Terminal, runs once an hour (6:40am–8:30pm).*

7 **Jeongsusa.** On the eastern slopes of Manisan is this temple, originally built during the Silla period. The original burned down, and it was later rebuilt in 1462 (during the Joseon Dynasty) and renamed the "clean water" temple. The doors are carved with a beautiful lotus-flower motif. *467-3 Sagi-ri,*

Ganghwa-do Practical Matters

From Seoul subway, take line 2 to Sinchon (exit 7) and catch a bus from the Sinchon Express Bus Terminal (5:40am–10pm; runs about every hour), which costs about ₩5,800. Alternately, take the Gang-hwa-do-bound bus from the Intercity Bus Terminal. The cheapest way (₩1,800) is to take the red long-distance bus from Sinchon (exit 1); walk past the Hyundai department store to the bus stop (across from the NH Bank). No. 3100 goes to Wonsu-ri, while no. 3000 goes to the Ganghwa Bus Terminal. Local buses loop around the top or the bottom areas of the island. Taxis are waiting nearby.

Two Ganghwa-do tours are offered by the city of Incheon. Starting at Incheon Station (10am–6pm), they cost ₩10,000 (you can't miss the starting point, the Tourist Info Center in front of the station). Course A covers: Ganghwa History Museum, the site of the Goryeo Royal Palace, Yongheunggung (a royal residence), Gang-hwa Pyeonghwa Observatory, Ganghwa Dolmen, and the ginseng center. Course B covers: Chojijin Fortress, Gwangseongbo Fort, Jeondeungsa, Seonwonsaji, Armiae World, and the ginseng center. For more details, check out http://english.ganghwa.incheon.kr, or call ☎ 02/930-3515.

Eating and Sleeping on Ganghwa-do

As it would stand to reason, Ganghwa-do is known for its sea-food, specifically its raw fish *(hwae)*, horse crabs *(ggotge)*, and grilled eel *(jang-uh gui)*. There are dozens of eel joints on the island, with a good grouping of them at the "Deorimi Eel Town" near Gang-hwa Bridge. The eel will be fresh and delicious but decidedly over-priced. For some of the spicy horse-crab stew or Korean sushi, there are a handful of restaurants near the Oepo-ri dock.

Though most people visit Ganghwa Island on a day trip, there is plenty here to warrant an overnight stay. There are several home-stays *(minbak)* and rental condos *(pensions)* on the island. Good options are the **Sea and Gallery Pension** (☎ 032/937-0416; www.sngpension.com) or **Dokmakvill Pension** (☎ 010/3286-8042; http://dongmakvill.com). The **Lotus Lantern International Meditation Center** (☎ 032/937-7033; www.lotuslantern.net), near Jeondeungsa, also offers temple stays on the first 3 weekends of the month.

Hwado-myeon, Ganghwa-gun, Incheon-si. ☎ 032/937-7372. Daily 24 hrs. Admission ₩3,000.

8 ★★ **Bomunsa.** Located on Seokmodo, a small island west of Ganghwa-do, it's known for its gorgeous views of the beach (especially at sunset) and the large sitting Buddha image carved on the rocky cliff. **Note:** No taxis are available on the island. 629 Mae-eum-ri, Samsan-myeon, Ganghwa-gun, Incheon-si.

☎ 032/933-8271. www.bomunsa.net (Korean only). Admission ₩2,000 adults, ₩1,500 teens, ₩1,200 children. Daily 9am–6pm. From Gang-hwa Bus Terminal, take bus to Oepo-ri and get off at Oepo-ri dock, and then take the ferry to Seokpo-ri (₩12,000 ages 13 and over, ₩600 ages 6–12 round-trip); from Seokpo-ri dock, take the bus to Bomunsa that runs hourly, 30 min. on weekends (7:15am–6:30pm).

Hiking outside Seoul.

Icheon

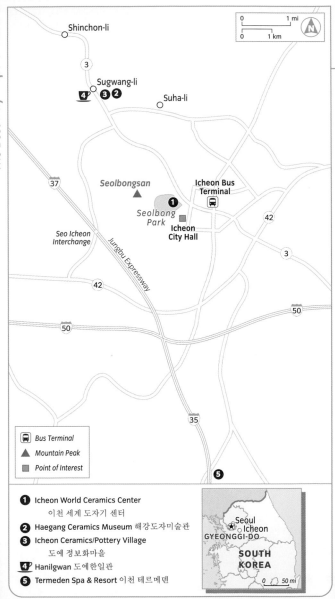

1 Icheon World Ceramics Center
이천 세계 도자기 센터
2 Haegang Ceramics Museum 해강도자미술관
3 Icheon Ceramics/Pottery Village
도예 정보화마을
4 Hanilgwan 도예한일관
5 Termeden Spa & Resort 이천 테르메덴

Less than an hour's drive away from Seoul is Icheon, the city of potters and rice. Since the Joseon Dynasty, the city has been the center of Korean ceramics. Located on some of the most fertile land in the country, this is where they grew the rice to feed the royal family. The town also sits on hot springs, which makes it an ideal stop for a visit to a water spa.

❶ ★★ Icheon World Ceramic Center. Run by the Korean Ceramics Foundation, it contains three permanent exhibition halls with more than 500 works by contemporary Korean and foreign ceramicists. While here, visit other attractions, like **Toya Land,** in Seolbong Park. 🕐 *2 hr. San 69-1 Gwanggo-dong.* ☎ *031/645-0693. www.wocef.com. Admission to the ceramic center is free, but admission to other attractions varies. Tues–Sun 9am–6pm.*

❷ ★ Haegang Ceramics Museum. Try to time your visit for when they're firing the kilns, since the small collection here may not be worth a special visit. Broken shards, victims of the traditional high temperature used during firing, surround the kilns. Some parts of the museum were under renovation when we visited, but the grounds and certain portions of the museum were still

Icheon World Ceramic Center.

open. 🕐 *1 hr. 330-1 Sugwang-ri, Sindun-myeon.* ☎ *031/634-2266. www.haegang.org (Korean only). Admission ₩2,000 adults, ₩1,000 children. Tues–Sun 9:30am–5:30pm.*

Icheon Practical Matters

Buses frequently travel to Icheon from DongSeoul Bus Terminal (in Gangbyeon) from 6:20am to 10:40pm, every 15 to 20 minutes. Buses from Seoul's Express Bus Terminal (in Gangnam) run 6:30am to 10pm daily, about every 30 to 50 minutes. They cost around ₩5,000 and take about an hour. If you're driving, take the Jungbu Expressway (no. 35) and get off at Icheon or Seo-Icheon toll exit.

    Plenty of taxis are available outside of Icheon Bus Terminal. The average cost to go to the kilns is about ₩5,000, or you can take one of the local buses (₩1,000). Bus no. 14 goes to Sindun myeon, where the majority of the kilns are located; it runs about every 10 minutes, and it's a 5-minute ride.

Kiln at Pottery Village.

❸ ★★★ Icheon Ceramics/Pottery Village. This is not really a "village" per se, but the kilns span the areas of Sugwang-ri, Sindun-myeon, and Saeum-dong. This "village" was a center of Korean traditional ceramics during the Joseon Dynasty. The artisans here still create celadon. The 300-plus active ceramics studios offer educational insight and hands-on classes for visitors. You can even buy the handiwork of some of Korea's "living cultural treasures." ⏱ *2 hr. No address, but studios span* *Sugwang-ri, Sindun-myeon, and Saeum-dong.* ☎ *031/644-2061.* *www.invil.org. Free admission. Mon–Sat 10am–5pm, but artisans have the weekends off.*

❹ ★★ Hanilgwan. The *ssal bap* (rice meal) comes with the usual 15 side dishes, but the *ingeum-nim ssal bap* (rice meal for a king) is affordable even for us commoners. *433 Sugwang2(i)-ri, Sindun-myeon.* ☎ *031/633-1400. Off national road no. 3. $$$.*

Termeden Spa.

5 ★★★ **kids** **Termeden Spa & Resort.** Pack your swimsuit and head for this large water park. It has a large wading pool with both indoor and outdoor sections where you can swim, soak, or get a water massage. You can also get actual massages for an additional fee, soak in an open-air spa, or scrub yourself in a Korean-style bath. During colder weather, you can also try the stone dry sauna, which feels a bit like being baked in a clay oven. ⏱ *2–3 hr. 372-7 Singal-ri, Moga-myeon.* ☎ *031/645-2000. www.termeden. com. Admission Mon–Fri ₩25,000 adults, ₩18,000 children; weekends and holidays ₩29,000 adults, ₩21,000 children; high season ₩39,000 adults, ₩28,000 children. Weekdays 8am–8pm; weekends 8am–9pm; longer hours during high season. Bus: From Icheon Bus*

Rice meal at Icheon.

Terminal, take bus no. 16-1 to Maok Nonghyup in Singal-ri.

Sleeping in Icheon

An overnight stay in Icheon will allow you a better chance to see the kilns when they are firing or special order a particular piece to be made by one of Korea's "living cultural treasures," the talented ceramists here. The largest hotel in the town, **Hotel Mirando** (☎ **031/633-2001;** www.mirandahotel.com) can't be missed. If you're visiting mostly for the spa, the sleeping quarters at the **Termeden Spa and Resort** (☎ **031/645-2000;** www.termeden.com) would be your best bet. The **Jisan Forest Resort** (☎ **031/330-1441;** www.jisangolf.com) has rooms for skiers and golfers, depending on the season. There are also a number of lower-priced motels and homestays around the bus terminal and a few in the ceramic villages. Rooms are readily available, except during the popular ceramics festival.

Types of Korean Ceramics

Korean ceramics became famous worldwide for their sophistication and artistry during the Goryeo Dynasty, when Korean potters learned the art of celadon from Chinese artisans. This light green pottery was created to emulate jade, which was super-popular and expensive at the time. Of course, Koreans also developed other types of ceramics, but all of them are characterized by the high heat of the kilns in which they are baked. The technique has a high attrition rate but, when successful, produces some beautiful results.

- **Celadon (*Cheongja*)**—Characterized by its green color and cracked glaze, this type of ceramics is highly prized by collectors. Today only a few artists create celadon in select small towns in South Korea. Of course, cheaper imitations are widely available.
- **Buncheong Ware (*Buncheong Sagi*)**—Made with a white slip painted over green pottery, this type of pottery was unique to Korea until the Pottery Wars, when the artisans were kidnapped and taken to Japan. When this form had almost completely disappeared from Korea, potters turned to white pottery.
- **Whiteware (*Baekja*)**—A process developed in 14th-century China, white pottery replaced celadon in popularity as Neo-Confucianists adopted simplicity in life as well as in their ceramics during the Joseon Dynasty. Korean whiteware is characterized by simplicity in design with symbolic images and much of the surface left white. There are only three places in South Korea where white pottery is still made: Namjong-myeon in Bunwon-li, Geumsa-li, and Gwangju-si.
- **Brown Earthenware (*Onggi*)**—This is the simplest form of utilitarian pottery, developed from the earliest forms of pottery. This dark-brown earthenware was used as everyday cooking and storage in kitchens of rich and poor alike. Even now, you will see traditional *hahng-ali* (clay bowls used for fermenting) holding chile paste or kimchi outside of traditional homes in the countryside. ●

Icheon pottery.

The
Savvy Traveler

Before You Go

Tourist Offices

Contact the **Korea Tourism Organization (KTO),** B1, 40 Cheonggyecheon-no (KTO Building [T2 Tower]), Jung-gu, Seoul 100-180 (☎ **02/7299-600;** http://english.visitkorea.or.kr; daily 9am–8pm), for a free visitors guide and map by mail. **Seoul's Foreign Language Services** can be reached by calling ☎ **02/120,** ext. 9 (http://english.seoul.go.kr). One of the best services the KTO provides is what it calls **Goodwill Guides.** These English-speaking volunteers (usually students, housewives, and the like) provide free translation and travel assistance. Visit the KTO website at least a week in advance of your trip, click on "Volunteer Tour Guides" in the "Essential Information" box on the left, and fill out a Goodwill Guide application. If you didn't do any advance planning, you can see which guides are available for the next 3 days. You can also call ☎ **011/123-1234** or e-mail goodwillguide@mail.knto.or.kr for additional assistance. The Tourist Assistance Center can be reached at ☎ **1330** (or from a cellphone at ☎ 02/1330).

The Best Times to Go

Spring and fall have the most pleasant weather. Summers are hot and humid with unpredictable rainfalls in July and August (typhoon season). Winters are dry with cold winds blowing down from Siberia. The city becomes a near ghost town during major Korean holidays like Seol (Lunar New Year) and Chuseok (Harvest Festival), when Seoulites leave town to visit family.

Previous page: Seoul has one of the most modern airports in the world.

Festivals and Special Events

Korea's traditional festivals follow the lunar calendar, but modern festivals follow the solar/Gregorian calendar.

WINTER The **Lunar New Year** (Seol or Seollal). The solar calendar equivalents for the next few years are January 23, 2012; February 10, 2013; January 31, 2014. Avoid traveling out of Seoul or be stuck in monumental traffic jams. Palaces and parks offer traditional games and performances. The days before and after are legal holidays.

SPRING The **Hi Seoul Festival** (☎ 02/3290-7150; www.hiseoulfest.org) happens a couple of times a year and celebrates the city's history and culture. Most events happen downtown. Don't miss the nighttime boat parade in Yeouido. Lasts about a week each season, with the largest festival in October. **The Icheon Ceramic Festival** (☎ 031/644-2944, ext. 4; www.ceramic.or.kr). Head to Icheon (see chapter 10) to experience the craftsmanship of Korean pottery firsthand. You can buy handmade ceramics directly from the artists. Late April. **The Lotus Lantern Festival** (☎ 02/2011-1744, ext. 8; www.llf.or.kr) celebrates the Buddha's Birthday (aka "The Day the Buddha Came"), and it is not to be missed. Thousands of people parade along the Han River with lanterns. The opening ceremony begins in front of the future Dongdaemun Design Center. Other events at Jogyesa and other temples in mid-May.

SUMMER Other than the **Hi Seoul Festival** (usually a week in early Aug), there are no annual events, but there's still plenty to do during the hot months in Seoul.

AVERAGE HIGH & LOW TEMPERATURE (°F/°C) & MONTHLY RAINFALL (INCHES) IN SEOUL

	JAN	FEB	MAR	APR	MAY	JUNE
Daily Temp. (°F)	36/23	40/27	50/36	65/46	73/55	81/65
Daily Temp. (°C)	2/-5	4/-3	10/2	18/8	23/13	27/18
Days of Precip.	0.7	0.9	1.3	2.1	3.1	4.6

	JULY	AUG	SEPT	OCT	NOV	DEC
Daily Temp. (°F)	84/72	86/72	79/63	68/50	54/39	40/28
Daily Temp. (°C)	29/22	30/22	26/17	20/10	12/4	4/-2
Days of Precip.	10.7	11.8	4	1.5	1.6	0.6

FALL **Chuseok** (Harvest Festival) is an important traditional holiday, held on the 15th day of the 8th lunar month. Although most Seoulites will be traveling to their ancestral homes, festivities are held at the palaces and at the National Folk Museum. Upcoming solar equivalents dates are September 12, 2011; September 30, 2012; September 19, 2013; and September 8, 2014. The days before and after are legal holidays. **The Icheon Rice Cultural Festival** (☎ 031/644-4121; www. ricefestival.or.kr) celebrates the rice grown in the plains of Icheon, which once grew the rice for Seoul's royalty. Stop in at a local restaurant for a rice meal. Held at Icheon's Seolbong Park. Late October.

The Weather

Seoul has four distinct seasons. Winters and summers are long with extreme temperatures, and the springs and autumns are short but lovely. Winter begins in November with a dry chill and very little snowfall. Spring starts by the end of March, and rainfall is unpredictable. By early June, heat and humidity move in with heavy rainfall that starts in July and sporadically goes through early September; 60% of the rain falls during the summer months. By late September, cool winds travel from the north. Autumn skies generally remain clear and crisp, with very

little rainfall. Koreans consider autumn the best season.

Cellphone (Mobile Phones)

Seoul (and all of South Korea) is on a CDMA network, so your unlocked GSM phone won't work here. The easiest way is to rent a phone. Two companies rent cellphones in Seoul. For both, you must reserve online (http://english.visitkorea.or.kr) before you arrive. **SK Telecom** (☎ 02/1566-2011) and **KTF Global Roaming Centers** (☎ 02/1588-0608) have locations in Incheon Airport. Phones cost ₩3,000 a day (or ₩2,000 if you sign up for a free membership at http://english.visit-korea.or.kr). Domestic calls cost ₩100 per 10 seconds; international rates vary. Fees do not include the 10% VAT.

Money Matters

Since South Koreans are avid credit card users, it's easy for visitors to use credit cards in most stores and restaurants. Visa and MasterCard are the most widely accepted, with some high-end hotels and restaurants accepting American Express. For smaller restaurants, outdoor markets, and bus fare, cash is necessary. However, don't carry an excessive amount. If you do, use a money belt since pickpockets may be lurking in the city's crowded subways and buses.

Currency

South Korea's official monetary unit is the won (₩). Currency is available in ₩10,000, ₩5,000, and ₩1,000 notes, and ₩500, ₩100, ₩50, and ₩10 coins (which are less in use). At the time this book went to press, the U.S. dollar was trading around ₩1,105, the pound sterling at ₩1,768, the euro at ₩1,505, the Canadian dollar at ₩1,113, and the Australian dollar at ₩1,093, and the New Zealand dollar at ₩854. Bear in mind that conversion rates may fluctuate depending on economic conditions. The latest rates can be found at **www.xe.com/ucc**.

Visa Requirements

British, Australian, and New Zealand citizens can visit for up to 90 days without a visa. Canadian citizens can visit for up to 90 days without a visa and can extend their stay for up to 6 months. U.S. and South African citizens visiting for fewer than 30 days do not require a visa. For trips up to 90 days, Americans need a C-3 short-term visitor visa. For short-term business trips (up to 90 days), you'll need a C-2 short-term business visa. Both are valid for multiple entries within a 5-year period (or until your passport expires). To get the visa, you'll need to file the application (available for download at **www.mofat.go.kr**), along with a photo and fee (generally $45 for U.S. citizens, though you should check the website to see if additional fees apply). Business travelers need an additional letter, invoice, or contract showing the nature of their business in South Korea. Submit visa applications by mail or in person to a South Korean embassy or consulate near you.

Getting **There**

By Plane

Most international flights fly into Seoul's Incheon Airport (ICN). The two South Korean airlines, **Korean Airlines** (www.koreanair.com) and **Asiana Airlines** (us.flyasiana.com), sometimes provide cheaper fares than their competition abroad. *Tip:* Try to book a flight that arrives before 10pm, since buses and subways stop running at midnight and taxi drivers take advantage by increasing fares.

Getting to & from the Airport

Special airport buses (called "limousine buses") are the easiest way to get to downtown Seoul. They run daily every 10 to 30 minutes, 5:30am until 10pm. A trip to downtown Seoul takes around 90 minutes (longer during rush hour). Limousine buses cost about ₩8,000, while KAL deluxe limousine buses cost ₩12,000 and stop at 20 of the major hotels.

Regular taxis charge around ₩40,000 to ₩60,000 to downtown Seoul. Deluxe taxis (they are black) charge around ₩65,000 to ₩90,000. Also, your taxi driver may make you pay the ₩7,100 toll charge for the expressway.

The **Airport Railroad (AREX)** connects Incheon to Gimpo Airport. From there you can take the subway to anywhere in the city. To get downtown from Gimpo via the subway, take line 5.

The AREX from Incheon Airport to Seoul Station started running in late 2010. The regular/commuter ride costs ₩5,300 and takes 53 minutes, including stops. The nonstop/express ride takes 43 minutes and costs ₩13,300. The commuter AREX takes T-money cards, while the express-train ticket can be purchased at the info desk next to the gates. Tickets for both lines can also be purchased at automated machines (cash only). Airline passengers (with tickets on Korean Air, Asiana, or Jeju Air) can check in

luggage, go through immigration, get screened at the newly built annex west of Seoul Station, and then proceed seven floors down to the AREX. Once at the airport, you get to go through a special section without having to go through airport security.

Getting **Around**

By Subway

Seoul is covered by an extensive metro system. The **Seoul Metro** (www.smrt.co.kr or www.nsubway.co.kr) is the best way to get around the city. Trains run 5:30am to midnight. Although you can buy single fares, it's better to buy a pass. The minimum fare is ₩1,000 or ₩900 with a **T-money card** (http://eng.t-money.co.kr), good for subways, buses, and even some taxis (the ones that have the CARD topper). Your best option is the **Seoul City Pass+** (www.seoulcitypass.com), which functions like a T-money card for tourists. With a base fee of ₩3,000, you can add value to the card in any amount from ₩1,000 to ₩90,000. If you're in Seoul for a brief time, the **Seoul City Pass** (www.seoulcitypass.com) may be a better option. You can board any bus or subway 20 times within a 24-hour period (ending at midnight), including unlimited on/off privileges on the **Seoul City Tour Bus** (the double-decker buses run by the city). One-day passes cost ₩15,000, 2-day ₩25,000, and 3-day ₩35,000.

By Bus

Unlike the streamlined subway system, **Seoul's buses** (☎ 02/414-5005; www.bus.go.kr, Korean only) can be confusing. Yet with more than 400 bus routes, the buses can take you pretty much anywhere. A

few buses have major destinations written in English, and occasional English announcements will be made at subway stations or major tourist destinations. Buses run daily from 5:30am to around midnight (a few routes go as late as 2am). Passes can be purchased at newsstands near bus stops, or you can use your T-money card or Seoul City Pass. The fare for **Express buses** is ₩1,100. **Ilban (regular) buses** (blue) and **maeul ("village") buses** (green) cost ₩1,000. The fares for long-distance (red) buses vary by destination.

By Taxi

You can flag down a taxi almost anywhere in Seoul. There are two types of taxis, and both are generally clean and safe. All taxis are metered with fares determined by distance and time. **Deluxe (mobeum) taxis,** which are black, cost more than regular taxis but can be more convenient since drivers speak basic English and accept credit cards. Tipping is not necessary, but it's a nice thing to do. Most passengers let the driver keep the change, at least.

By Car

Driving around Seoul is not recommended, since drivers are aggressive and parking is difficult. If you must, you can rent a car starting at around ₩70,000 per day. You have to be at least 21 years old and have an International Driving Permit (IDP), which you must get in your home country before you leave. In the U.S., there are only two authorized organizations that provide IDPs—the **American Automobile Association** (**AAA**; www.aaa.com) and **the National Automobile Club** (☎650/294-7000). The best place to rent a car is at Incheon Airport. Check prices at **Kumho** (www.kumhorent.com) or **Avis** (www.avis.co.kr). A safer option is to rent both a car and a driver, which costs about ₩75,000 for 3 hours and ₩142,000 for 10 hours. You can arrange this through Kumho or Avis, or through most high-end hotels.

Fast **Facts**

BUSINESS HOURS Banks: Monday to Friday 9am to 4pm. **Major department stores:** Daily 10:30am to 8pm with extended weekend hours. **Smaller shops:** Hours vary, but usually early morning to late evening; stores catering to younger people generally stay open until 10pm; convenience stores often stay open until midnight. **Restaurants:** Most open daily from 10am to 10pm. **Government offices (including tourist info):** Monday to Friday 9am to 6pm (until 5pm Nov–Feb), Saturday 9am to 1pm.

CONSULATES AND EMBASSIES The following embassies are in Seoul: **United States** (☎ 02/397-4114; http://seoul.usembassy.gov), **United Kingdom** (☎ 02/3210-5500; http://ukinkorea.fco.gov.uk/en), **Canada** (☎ 02/3783-6000; www.korea.gc.ca), and **Australia** (☎ 02/2003-0100; www.southkorea.embassy.gov.au).

DENTISTS Lucky for you, many dentists in Seoul were trained in colleges in the U.S., and some speak very good English, especially those in Itaewon and Gangnam. A good bet is **Dr. Choi and Associates,** 2F, 726-173 Hannam-dong (Volvo Bldg.), Yongsan-gu (☎ **02/796-2224;** www.dentasso.com; subway line 6 to Hangangjin Station), or **Tufts Dental,** 437 Teheran-ro, Ste. 302, Gangnam-gu (☎ **02/553-7512;** www.tuftsdental.net).

ELECTRICITY Seoul is on a 220-volt, 60-cycle system (the plugs with two round prongs), but a few major hotels have 110-volt, 60-cycle systems. Check before plugging in any electronics. It's very difficult to find universal plug adapters, so it's best to buy one before you arrive.

EMERGENCIES Dial ☎ **112** anywhere in the country for the police. Dial ☎ **119** for the fire and medical emergencies, or ☎ **1339** for medical emergencies (most operators speak only Korean).

HOSPITALS These hospitals have international clinics: Samsung Medical Center (☎ 02/3410-0200), Sinchon Severance (☎ 02/361-6540), Asan Medical Center (☎ 02/2224-3114), Kangbuk Samsung Medical Center (☎ 02/723-2911), Hannam-dong International Medical Center (☎ 02/790-0857), Seoul Foreign Clinic (☎ 02/796-1871), Samsung First Medical Center (☎ 02/2262-7071), Yeouido Catholic Medical Center (☎ 02/789-1114), Gangnam Catholic Medical Center (☎ 02/590-1114), CHA General Hospital (☎ 02/3468-3127), Soonchunhyang Hospital (☎ 02/709-9881), and Seoul National University Hospital (☎ 02/760-2890).

MAIL Post offices can be easily spotted by their red signs with a white symbol of three stylized swallows on it, and they say POST OFFICE in English. They're open 9am to 6pm Monday to Friday (until 5pm Nov–Feb). Airmail to North America takes about 5 to 10 days, but delays are not uncommon. For sending packages overseas, try **UPS** (☎ **02/1588-6886;** www.ups.com), **Federal Express** (☎ **080/023-8000;** www.fedex.com/kr_english), or **DHL** (☎ **02/716-0001;** www.dhl.co.kr).

SMOKING Although South Korea has one of the highest smoking rates in the world, the government has been aggressive in its antismoking campaign. Smoking is banned in public buildings, hospitals, schools, subways, bus stops, office hallways, stadiums, and restrooms. You can smoke outside or in designated smoking rooms. Restaurants, cafes, Internet cafes, and large establishments are required to provide nonsmoking areas, though many don't. If you're caught violating the smoking ban, you may be fined ₩20,000 to ₩30,000.

TAXES Value-added tax (VAT) is levied on most goods and services at the standard 10% rate and usually included in the retail price. You can receive a refund on your VAT if you purchase your item at a shop with a TAX-FREE SHOPPING sign. Ask for a Global Refund Cheque payment slip at the time of your purchase. You can get your refund, within 3 months of purchase, at the Cash Refund Office at Gate 28 of Incheon Airport.

TIPPING Tipping is not customary in South Korea, but feel free to do so if you've received extraordinary service. In most tourist hotels, a 10% service charge is added to your bill (on top of the VAT). In some high-end restaurants, a 3% to 10% service charge may be added to your bill. When riding a taxi, it's not necessary to tip the driver, but do let him keep the change.

TOILETS There are free public restrooms in most subway stations, bus terminals, train stations, and tourist attractions. However, they vary from the usual Western-style toilets to the traditional squat toilets on the floor. Since not all of them provide toilet paper or paper towels, it's best to carry a small packet of tissues with you. You can buy them at any corner store or in vending machines outside some restrooms for about ₩500. American-style fast-food restaurants, department stores, large bookstores, and hotels have the best public restrooms.

WATER Drinking tap water in Seoul is not recommended. Filtered or bottled water is always available in restaurants, and you can buy bottles at convenience stores, usually for about ₩500 apiece.

A Brief **History**

Archaeological evidence shows that humans had been living along the Han River since the Paleolithic period and settled in what is now Seoul during the Neolithic Age. Visitors can see evidence of human life some 3,000 to 7,000 years ago at the Amsa Prehistoric Site in Gangdong-gu. However, Seoul's importance as a capital city did not begin until the Three Kingdoms period.

18 B.C. Baekje declares Wiryeseong its capital (inside what is now Seoul).

A.D. **392** Control of Wiryeseong passes to Goguryeo as that kingdom takes over the area.

551 Baekje and Silla form an alliance and take control of the capital region.

668–935 Unified Silla take over. The Korean peninsula is under one government for the first time.

1104 King Sukjong of the Goryeo Dynasty chooses Yangju (present-day Seoul) as one of the "three small capitals" of the kingdom and builds a palace there, calling it Namgyeong (the "Southern Capital").

1394 King Yi Seong-gye of the Joseon Dynasty moves the capital to present-day Seoul and calls it Hanyang.

1395 King Yi builds palaces, royal shrines, and a fortified wall surrounding the city and calls it Hanseong (which means "fortress city on the Han River"). The entire city was surrounded by a stone fortress 20 feet (6m) high to provide security from thieves, attackers, and tigers.

1660S The population of Seoul is about 200,000 and remains steady.

1890S The Korean government opens the country (and the city) to foreigners, and the population of the city begins increasing for the first time in nearly 200 years.

1910 Japan invades Korea and makes Seoul its colonial capital. The city became known as Gyeongseongbu.

1945 At the end of World War II, Korea is liberated from the Japanese and the city gets its current name, Seoul.

1948 Seoul is designated the capital of the newly established Korean government. The city has nine districts ("gu") and a population of nearly 1.4 million.

1950 Civil war breaks out between the Chinese-backed north and UN-backed south. Control of the city goes back and forth four times during the Korean War, reducing it to rubble. At the end of the war, the damaged city had a population of 2.5 million, half of whom were homeless refugees from the north.

1953 After the signing of the Armistice Agreement ending fighting of the Korean War, Seoul becomes the capital of the newly formed Republic of Korea.

1962 Seoul Metropolitan Government is put under the direct control of the Prime Minister, giving it autonomy with less direct supervision from the national government.

1963 Seoul incorporates the area south of the Han River to increase its administrative district and expand its territory.

1973 Seoul expands its territory again to incorporate more parts of Gyeonggi-do.

1988 Seoul hosts the Summer Olympic Games.

1994 Seoul celebrated its 600th year as a capital city.

2002 Seoul co-hosts the FIFA World Cup with Japan.

2010 Seoul hosts the G20 Summit.

TODAY Seoul is home to more than 10 million people, nearly a quarter of South Korea's population. It has 25 gu (districts) and 522 dong ("villages") in just over 376 square miles (974 sq km).

Etiquette & Customs

Korean society is largely based on Confucian ideals, which means that it is a patriarchal society and there is deep respect for family and elders. In business and social settings, age and social ranking are considered of utmost importance. Although foreigners aren't necessarily bound by the same rules as natives, it's always best to respect people's customs.

Appropriate Attire: South Korea is still generally a conservative society and very revealing clothes are considered inappropriate. It's best to leave clothes like crop-tops, flip-flops, and miniskirts at home. This is especially true when visiting a temple or going to the DMZ. Also remember that you should always take off your shoes when visiting a Korean home or entering a temple. If you're a woman traveling in the summertime, be sure to carry a pair of socks in your purse so that you're not walking around someone's home barefoot, which is considered a bit rude.

Avoiding Offense: Respecting others according to seniority, age, or social status is a huge part of Korean society. Koreans believe that direct eye contact during conversations shows boldness, so too much direct eye contact should be avoided. When given something by an older person, accept it with both hands. Also, young people shouldn't lie around, wear sunglasses, or smoke in front of an elder. On public transportation, younger people are expected to give up their seats for the elderly (foreigners aren't expected to do this, but it's the polite thing to do). Although it's changing a bit, women who smoke in public are considered to be loose. Never write anyone's name in red ink. It's like saying that

person is dead, or that he or she will die soon. In Korea, a person's surname is written first and first names are rarely used for elders or people of higher social ranking.

Photography: When taking photos of people, ask permission. It's not that Koreans object to being photographed, it's just the polite thing to do. Some places will restrict photography (usually indicated with a picture of a camera with an X through it). For instance, it is considered inappropriate to take a photo of the main Buddha image in a temple. Remember, just because you see others doing it, doesn't mean it's okay. And don't ever use a flash when taking pictures of monks who are in prayer.

Photography is restricted at the DMZ. Don't take pictures of any soldiers or military facilities under any circumstances.

Eating & Drinking: Dining is usually a family or group affair in Korea. The eldest or most senior person at the table eats first. No one should even pick up his or her chopsticks until the eldest has taken a bite. If you're the guest of honor or the senior at the table, everyone is waiting for you, so don't linger. Everyone gets his or her own bowl of rice (and sometimes soup) and can help him or herself to any number of shared dishes, so don't worry about reaching in front of someone or asking for a dish to be passed. Koreans traditionally eat rice with the spoon and everything else with chopsticks.

During the meal, rest your chopsticks and spoon on top of a dish (or the lid for your bowl of rice, if you have one). Don't stick your chopsticks or spoon in a bowl of rice—this is only done during *jesa* (ancestral memorial ceremonies).

When you are finished, you can rest your implements on the table, to show that you're done. It is considered rude to blow your nose or to cough at the table—excuse yourself from the table first.

During a meal, never lick your fingers; it's considered uncouth. However, when eating noodles or soup, slurping isn't considered rude. Koreans pour drinks for one another. It's considered bad etiquette to pour your own drink, especially before pouring for others. Hold the glass with two hands when someone's pouring; then return the favor by pouring the other person's drink.

Tipping is not done in restaurants or otherwise (although it's customary to let the taxi driver keep the change). Most hotels and upscale restaurants will include the service charge (usually 10%) on your bill.

Religion in Seoul

The oldest religious ideas in Korea are shamanism and animism. Adherents believed that the natural world was filled with both helpful and harmful spirits that could be communicated with by special people, called shamans. Most shamans were women, and certain dances, chants, and herbal remedies marked their beliefs. Although very few people practice this religion today, most Koreans still use herbal remedies, and shamanistic dances and chants can be seen in traditional performances.

Buddhism made its way into Korea through monks who traveled from central Asia, across China, into the peninsula in about A.D. 372. The new religion was allowed to blend in with the shamanistic beliefs at the time. The mountains that were believed to be homes to the spirits became sites of Buddhist temples.

Chinese monks brought Mahayana Buddhism with them. Korean Buddhism is a form of this religion, except that they tried to resolve what they saw as internal inconsistencies. This new approach, founded by monk Wonhyo, was called Tong Bulgyo (Interpenetrated Buddhism).

Buddhism was the predominant religion during the Three Kingdoms period and became the official state religion under Unified Silla. With the king's support, many temples were built in subsequent centuries (thousands of them, rebuilt after wars and fires, still exist today). One unique feature of Korean temples is a small chapel on the side of the main hall, dedicated to a mountain spirit. Usually depicted as an old man with a pet tiger, it is a symbol of native shamanistic beliefs and an attempt to appease local mountain spirits on whose land the temple stands.

Buddhism continued its popularity as the state religion throughout the Goryeo period. However, as the Joseon Dynasty came into power on the peninsula, Neo-Confucian ideology overtook the Buddhist faith. Monks fled major towns and found enclaves in hidden mountain temples. Only after warrior monks helped defend against the Japanese Hideyoshi invasion did the government end its persecution against Buddhists. However, the religion remained subdued until the end of the Joseon period, when it gained more strength during the Japanese occupation.

Today many factions of Buddhism exist in South Korea since Buddhism is not a centralized religion. Popular are Seon (which became Zen in Japan)

Buddhism; Taego, a modern revival of Cheontae; and the more contemporary Won Buddhism. It's still a bit odd in modern society to see a monk in his gray robes talking on a cellphone, but within the different factions, some monks are allowed to marry and have worldly goods. About 45% of the Korean population is Buddhist.

Confucianism, although not a religion, has had the greatest influence on Korean culture. It was an important part of government systems starting from the 7th century A.D. and became the official system of belief in the 14th century A.D., during the Joseon Dynasty. Its philosophical systems are still part of the undercurrent of Korean society.

Christianity came to the peninsula when Roman Catholic missionaries arrived in 1794 (although Jesuit writings were brought into Korea more than a century prior).

Mostly because Catholic converts refused to perform Confucian ancestral rites, the government prohibited Christianity. Some early converts were executed during the early 19th century, but anti-Christian laws were not strictly enforced. By the 1860s, there were thousands of Roman Catholics in the country, which caused the government to start their persecution. Subsequently, thousands of Catholics were killed.

In the 1880s, Protestant missionaries and more Catholic priests came to Korea, converting a large number of the population. During the Japanese occupation, Christians played a significant role in the country's struggle for independence. After World War II, Catholicism grew rapidly, but Protestantism grew faster. Christianity has now become the majority religion in the country.

Recommended **Books, Films** & **Music**

Books

Although classic texts and popular English-language literature are often translated into Korean, the reverse is not true. Very few Korean books are translated into English. However, the newer generations of Korean immigrants, foreign-born Koreans, and non-Koreans are writing interesting books about the culture.

Nonfiction books on Korea include the following: **20th Century Korean Art** (2005) by Youngna Kim is a solid introduction to contemporary works by current artists. **Korean Folk Art and Craft** (1993) by Edward B. Adams, although a bit dated, is an excellent guide to understanding Korea's folk objects. **Korea's Place in the Sun: A Modern History**

(2005, updated edition) by Bruce Cumings is an excellent overview of the history of the peninsula. **Korea Style** (2006) by Marcia Iwatate and Kim Unsoo is perhaps the only book in English about Korean architectural and interior design, highlighting 22 homes in the country. **Eating Korean: From Barbecue to Kimchi, Recipes from My Kitchen** (2005) is a friendly guide to Korean cuisine. Written by the author of this guide, it includes personal stories and more than 100 recipes. **Quick and Easy Korean Cooking** (2009), also written by this book's author, introduces Korean flavors into your home kitchen.

There are some good Korean fictional works translated into English, although some are only available in limited release: Kim Young-ha's debut novel, *I Have a Right to Destroy Myself* (1996/2007), catapulted the writer to South Korean and international fame. The novel, which is about a young man in modern-day South Korea who helps his clients commit suicide, provides well-written insight into the psychology of some residents of Seoul. It won him the Munhak-dongne prize the year it was published. His subsequent novels were also quite celebrated, including his latest, *Your Republic Is Calling You* (2006/2010), a tale of a North Korean spy, who has lived undercover in Seoul for 21 years, only to be called back to Pyongyang.

Between Heaven and Earth (1996/2002), by Yun Dae-nyeong, was the winner of the Yi Sang Literature Prize in 1996. It's a story about a transient relationship between a man on his way to a funeral and a woman he meets on the way. *The Wings* (2001) by Yi Sang is a collection of three semiautobiographical short stories on life, love, and death. *The Rainy Spell* (1973/2002) by Yun Heung-gil is an incredibly touching and sad story about the Korean War. *House of Idols* (1960/1961/1966/2003) by Cho In-hoon is about two soldiers in Seoul after the Korean War. It includes "End of the Road," a story about a prostitute around a U.S. military base. *It's Hard to Say: Buddhist Stories Told by Seon Master Daehaeng* (2005) is an illustrated introduction to Seon (Zen) teachings, with fun stories for adults and children.

Films

Since the late '90s, South Korean films have been gaining international recognition and winning prizes at festivals worldwide. Though not comprehensive by any means, the following is a list of films I found notable in the past decade or so.

Oki's Film (2010) is Hong Sang-soo's latest play on narrative, using different POVs to tell the same story. Also the same year, Hong's *Hahaha* also plays with the idea of narrator, but this time within the setting of two friends catching up over drinks. His older *Tale of Cinema* (2005) garnered him international recognition at the Cannes Film Festival, but Hong's *Like You Know It All* (2009) and *Night and Day* (2008) are also worth a look, if you like his brand of humor and storytelling.

The President's Last Bang (2005), directed by Im Sang-soo, is a controversial political satire dramatizing the last days of President Park Chung-hee. His military dictatorship ended in 1979 with his assassination by his own men. The Korean title translates literally to *Those People at That Time*.

Oasis (2002), an award-winning film by Lee Chang-dong, is about a relationship between an ex-convict and a woman with cerebral palsy. The brilliant acting by Moon So-ri garnered her the Marcello Mastroianni Award at Venice that year.

Chunhyang (2000) is a period drama about two lovers in 18th-century Korea, beautifully told by one of the country's best-known directors, Im Kwon-Taek. The story reveals the historical reality and stark class differences prevalent at that time.

Farewell, My Darling (1996), written and directed by Park Cheol-Su (director of *301/302*), is about a family mourning the death of its patriarch. It is an excellent commentary on the contradictions and commingling of Confucius traditions and modern life in Korea.

Music

You may have heard of the KPop sensation Rain (real name Jeong Ji-hoon) or seen him in such films as *Speed Racer* or *Ninja Assassin*.

Although he may be the most internationally famous, there are plenty of other KPop groups popular in South Korea. Of these, female vocalist Boa is one of the few who have been able to make a crossover album in English. Still, South Korean pop singers and performers quickly rise and fall. Kpopmusic.com is a good source for checking out the latest hits and bands.

Despite the temporary nature of today's pop music in South Korea, the country's musical roots go back centuries, back to its shamanistic roots. Korea's traditional music grew from some outside influences (for example, Buddhism) but has its own origins. Special court music and ensembles were performed for royalty and aristocrats. These date back to the beginning of the Joseon Dynasty, but it's very rare to catch a court music performance these days, aside from special events put on by the National Center for Korean Traditional Performing Arts.

On the other end of the spectrum were the folk musicians, who traveled from town to town putting on impromptu concerts for commoners. The villagers would throw the roving musician a few coins or feed them in return for the entertainment.

Pungmul is a type of folk music tradition that grew from shamanistic rituals and Korea's agricultural society. A pungmul performance is led by drumming, but it includes wind instruments as well as dancers. Because it's a kinetic, colorful performance, a recording of pungmul music rarely does it justice. However, *samul nori*, which also has its roots in *nongak* (farmer's music), makes use of four of the drums found in pungmul. Each drum represents various elements of weather—rain, wind, clouds, and thunder. It's a good entry into

Korean traditional music, especially for those who like percussion.

Pansori is one of the most famous types of traditional performance. Sometimes called the Korean "blues" (not because of the style but more of the sadness in the music), pansori is a long, drawn-out performance by one singer and one accompanying drummer. The lyricist tells a narrative song, inviting audience participation and joke-telling along the way.

Sanjo (which translates literally as "scattered melodies") is one of the most advanced forms of Korean music. It describes a solo performance on a traditional instrument in which the performer begins slowly but builds up to a faster, more spontaneous tempo, adding improvisations and showing off his or her skills with each successive movement. In an entirely instrumental performance, the rhythms shift as the performance progresses.

There are *sanjo* for *piri* (bamboo oboe), *daegeum* (bamboo flute), *haegeum* (two-string bowed instrument), *ajaeng* (bowed zither), *geomungo* (six-stringed zither), and the *gayageum* (12-string zither).

One of my favorite modern gayageum masters is **Hwang Byungki** (www.bkhwang.com), who has played both traditional and original compositions on the Korean zither. His album *The Labyrinth* (2003) contains some of the most experimental of his works, while *Spring Snow* (2001) is a more meditative and minimal presentation.

A celebrated performer of the daegeum is **Lee Saeng-gang** (www.leesaengkang.com, Korean only). His album *Daegeum Sori* (2007) is an excellent introduction to the sounds of the bamboo flute, but his *Sound of Memory Vol. 2* is a more haunting study of the daegeum.

Korean Alphabet Guide

The Korean alphabet (Hangeul) has 24 letters—14 consonants and 10 vowels. It is a syllabary, which means that no letter can stand alone. At least one vowel and at least one consonant are combined to make a syllable. In the book, I try to make the spelling as close to how Korean sounds when read by English speakers, while using the Korean government's spelling for the most part.

The Consonants
ㄱ   A cross between "g" and "k," pronounced like in the word "go," now spelled with the letter "g" (old spelling was "k")

ㄲ   A double consonant, the sound of a hard "g" or "k" as in the Spanish word queso, spelled "gg" or "kk"

ㄴ   Pronounced the same as "n"

ㄷ   A cross between "d" and "t," as in "dark," spelled with a "d" (old spelling: "t")

ㄸ   A double consonant, the sound of a hard "d/t" as in the Spanish word tio or the "t" in "study," spelled with "dd"

ㄹ   A cross between "r" and "l," similar to the Spanish gracias, spelled with an "l" or "r"

ㅁ   Pronounced like the letter "m"

ㅂ   A cross between the letters "b" and "p," like the "b" in "boar," spelled with the letter "b" (old spelling "p")

ㅃ   A double consonant, the sound of a hard "b" or "p" as in the Spanish name Pepe, spelled "bb"

ㅅ   Similar to the letter "s," except when it's at the end of a syllable with a consonant following in the next syllable; then, it's pronounced with a short "t" sound

ㅆ   A double consonant, the sound of a hard "s" as in the word "sour," spelled with "ss"

ㅇ   At the beginning of a syllable, it allows the vowel to be sounded without a hard consonant sound. At the end of a syllable, it sounds like "ng," as in the end of the word "song."

ㅈ   Pronounced like the letter "j" in "jazz" (old spelling "ch")

ㅉ   A double consonant, the sound of a hard "j," spelled with "jj"

ㅊ   Pronounced like "ch" in "choice"

ㅋ   Pronounced like "k"

ㅌ   Pronounced like "t"

ㅍ   Pronounced like "p"

ㅎ   Pronounced like "h"

The Vowels
ㅏ   Pronounced like "ah," as in "spa"

ㅑ   Pronounced "ya"

ㅓ   Pronounced "uh," as in "umbrella," spelled "eo"

ㅕ   Pronounced "yuh," as in "yum," spelled "yeo"

ㅗ   Pronounced "oh," as in "rope"

ㅛ   Pronounced "yo"

ㅜ   Pronounced "ooh," as in "stew," often spelled "u" or sometimes "oo"

ㅠ   Pronounced "yu," as in "you," spelled "yu" or "yoo"

— Pronounced "eu," as in "good" or "hood"
ㅣ Pronounced "ee," as in "see"
ㅔ A combination vowel pronounced "eh"
ㅒ A combination vowel pronounced "ye," as in "yes"
ㅘ A combination vowel pronounced "wa"
ㅞ A combination vowel pronounced "whe," as in "sweat"
ㅝ A combination vowel pronounced "wuh," as in "was"
ㅟ A combination vowel pronounced "wee"
ㅢ A combination vowel pronounced "eui" (but said quickly)

Korean Language Guide

GREETINGS & INTRODUCTIONS

ENGLISH	PRONUNCIATION	KOREAN
Hello, how are you?	Ahn nyeong hasehyo? (formal)	안녕하세요.
Hello/good-bye. (informal)	Ahn nyeong.	안녕.
Hello. (on the telephone)	Yuh boh seh yo.	여보세요.
Good-bye. (when you're leaving)	Ahn nyong hi geh seh yo.	안녕히계세요.
Good-bye. (when you're staying)	Ahn nyong hi gah seh yo.	안녕히가세요.
Yes	ye or ne	예 or 네
No	ahniyo	아니오
Thank you.	Gahm sah hamnida. (formal)	감사합니다.
	Goh mab seumnida. (less formal)	고맙습니다.
You're welcome.	Cheonmahneyo.	천만에요.
I'm sorry./Excuse me.	Jeh sohng hamnida. (formal)	죄송합니다.
	Mi ahn hamnida. (less formal)	미안합니다.
Pleased to meet you.	Mannaseo bahngapseumnida. (formal)	만나서 반갑습니다.
	Mannaseo bangaweoyo. (less formal)	만나서 반가워요.

NUMBERS

Koreans have two ways of counting. One system is based on the Chinese counting method, and the other is the traditional Korean way. In general, the system from the Chinese is used to count objects and money, and the Korean system is used to count people.

ENGLISH	PRONUNCIATION	KOREAN
1	il	일
2	ee	이
3	sahm	삼
4	sah	사
5	oh	오
6	yook	육
7	chil	칠
8	pahl	팔
9	gu	구
10	ship	십
11	shibil (combine 10 and 1)	십일
12	shibee (and so forth)	십이
20	ee ship (combine 2 and 10)	이십
30	sam ship (combine 3 and 10)	삼십
100	baek	백
200	ee baek (combine 2 and 100)	이백
1,000	chun	천
2,000	ee cheon (combine 2 and 1000)	이천
10,000	mahn	만
20,000	ee mahn (combine 2 and 10,000)	이만
100,000	shipmahn (combine 10 and 10,000)	십만
200,000	ee shipmahn (combine 20 and 10,000)	이십만
1,000,000	baek mahn (combine 100 and 10,000)	백만

USEFUL QUESTIONS & PHRASES

ENGLISH	PRONUNCIATION	KOREAN
When?	Uhnje imnikka?	언제입니까?
Where is it?	Uhdi imnikka?	어디입니까?
Where are you?	Uhdieh isseubnikka?	어디에 있습니까?
Who is it?	Noo goo shipnikka?	누구십니까?
What is it?	Mueo shimnikka?	무엇입니까?
What is this?	Ee guh seun mueo shimnikka?	이것은무엇입니까?
How much is it?	Uhl mah imnikka?	얼마입니까?
Where is the bathroom?	Hwa jang shili uh di imnikka?	화장실이 어디입니까?
Do you speak English?	Yeongeo halsu isseumnikka?	영어할수있읍니까?
What is your name?	Ileumi mueo shimnikka?	이름이무엇입니까?
My name is. . .	Je ileum eun. . . imnida.	제이름은. . . 입니다.
I don't understand.	Ihae mot hamnida.	이해못합니다.
I don't know.	Jal moleu gaesseumnida.	잘모르겠습니다.
Please wait a moment.	Jamsi mahn gidalyeo jooseyo.	잠시만 기다려주세요.

TIME

ENGLISH	PRONUNCIATION	KOREAN
Time	shigahn	시간
morning	ahchim	아침
a.m.	ohjeon	오전
afternoon/lunch	jeom shim	점심
p.m.	ohhu	오후
evening/dinner	jeonyuk	저녁
night	bahm	밤
minute	boon	분
second	cho	초
now	jigeum	지금
today	ohneul	오늘
yesterday	eohjae	어제
tomorrow	naeil	내일
1 hour	han shigan	한시간
5 hours	dahseot shigan	다섯시간
Monday	Weolyeo-il	월요일
Tuesday	Hwayeo-il	화요일
Wednesday	Suyeo-il	수요일
Thursday	Mogyeo-il	목요일
Friday	Geumyeo-il	금요일
Saturday	Toyeo-il	토요일
Sunday	Ilyeo-il	일요일
weekday	jujung	주중
weekend	jumal	주말

TRANSPORTATION

ENGLISH	PRONUNCIATION	KOREAN
taxi	tekshi	택시
car	cha	차
parking	jucha	주차
bus	buhseu	버스
express bus	gosok/jwaseok	고속/좌석
bus terminal	beoseu teominal	버스털미날
city bus	shinae beoseu	시내버스
subway	jihacheol/jeoncheol	지하철/전철
train	gicha	기차
boat	beh	배
airplane	biheng-gi	비행기
airport	biheng-jang/gohng-hahng	비행장/공항
entrance	ipgu	입구
exit	choolgu	출구
ticket	pyo	표
Do you go to. . . ?	. . .ga-seyo?	. . .가세요?
Is there a bus to. . . ?	. . .ganeun buseu isseumnikka?	. . .가는 버스 있읍니까?
What times does it leave?	Myeotshi-ae chulbal hamnikka?	몇시에출발합니까?

ENGLISH	PRONUNCIATION	KOREAN
What times does it arrive?	Myeotshi-ae dochak hamnikka?	몇시에도착합니까?
How long does it take?	Uhlmahnna geollimnikka?	얼마나걸립니까?
Please take me to. . .	. . .eulo gajooseyo.	. . .으로주세요
Please let me know when we arrive.	Dochak ha-myeon allyeojooseyo.	도착하면알려주세요.
Please stop here.	Yeogiseo sewojooseyo.	여기서세워주세요.

NAVIGATION

ENGLISH	PRONUNCIATION	KOREAN
north	buk	북
south	nam	남
east	dong	동
west	seo	서
left	wenjjok/jwacheuk	왼쪽/좌측
right	oleunjjok/ucheuk	오른쪽/우측
turn left	jwahwaejeon	좌회전
turn right	oohwaejeon	우회전
go straight	jigjin	직진
four-way	sa-geoli	사거리
here	yuhgi	여기
there	guhgi	거기
over there	juhgi (indicating something farther)	저기
Is it close by?	Gakkapseumnikka?	가깝습니까?

MONEY

ENGLISH	PRONUNCIATION	KOREAN
₩500	oh baek won	오백원
₩1,000	cheon won	천원
change	jahn dohn	잔돈
Do you have change?	Jahn dohn isseumnikka?	잔돈있읍니까?

SHOPPING PHRASES

ENGLISH	PRONUNCIATION	KOREAN
What is this?	Ee guh seun mueo shimnikka?	이것은무엇입니까?
How much is it?	Uhl mah imnikka? (formal)	얼마입니까?
	Uhl mah eh yo? (more informal)	얼마에요?
It's too expensive.	Neomu bissayo.	너무비싸요.
Please give me a deal.	Ssage haejooseyo.	싸게해주세요.
May I try it on? (clothes)	Ibeoh bolsu innayo?	입어볼수있나요?
May I try it on? (shoes)	Shineoh bolsu innayo?	신어볼수있나요?
Please give me that./ I'll take this.	Igeoseul jusipsiyo.	이것을 주십시요.

ENGLISH	PRONUNCIATION	KOREAN
Please give me only one.	Hana-mahn jooseyo.	하나만 주세요.
Do you take credit cards?	Shinyong kadeu bahdseubnikka?	신용카드 받습니까?
I need a receipt.	Yeong-su-jeung pilyeo hamnida.	영수증 필요합니다.
Please wrap it for me.	Pojang-heh jooseyo.	포장해주세요

ACCOMMODATIONS

ENGLISH	PRONUNCIATION	KOREAN
Hotel	hotel	호텔
motel	motel	모텔
homestay	minbak	민박
room	bahng	방
bed	chimdae	침대
reservation	yeyak	예약
laundromat	setakso	세탁소
Where is a cheap hotel?	Ssan hoteli eodi isseumnikka?	싼호텔이 어디있습니까?
How much for 1 night?	Halu ulma-imnikka?	하루 얼마입니까?
Could you wake me up at. . . ?	. . .eh ggaewuh jooseyo?	. . .깨워주세요?

RESTAURANT

ENGLISH	PRONUNCIATION	KOREAN
May I see the menu, please?	Menyu jom boyeo jooseyo?	메뉴 좀보여주세요?
What is your best dish?	Ijibeseo jalhaneun eum-sikgi mueosijyo?	이집에서 잘하는 음식 이 무엇이죠?
Do you have. . . ?	. . .issuh-yo?	. . .있어요?
Please bring some more of this.	Igut jogeum duh jooseyo.	이것, 조금 더 주세요.
More rice, please.	Bapduh jooseyo.	밥 더 주세요.
Is this spicy?	I-gesseun maewuh-yo?	이것은 매요?
Don't make it spicy.	Mepji-ankeh he-jooseyo.	맵지않게해주세요.
I'm a vegetarian.	Chaeshik ju-eija imnida.	채식주의자입니다.
water	mool	물
beer	maekju	맥주
soda	eumnyosu	음료수
tea	cha	차
coffee	kuhpi	커피
chopsticks	jutgalak	젓가락
spoon	sootgalak	숟가락
toothpick	issooshigae	이쑤시개
Please bring me the bill.	Gaesan he-jooseyo.	계산해주세요.
I enjoyed the meal./ I ate well.	Jal muguh seumnida.	잘먹었습니다.

Seoul Menu Reader

A Korean meal usually is made with balance in mind—hot and cool, spicy and mild, yin and yang. At the core of every meal is *bap* (rice), unless the meal is noodle- or porridge-based. Koreans don't distinguish among breakfast, lunch, or dinner, so it's not unusual to eat rice three times a day.

In addition to individual bowls of rice, you may get a single serving of soup. Hot pots (*jjigae* or *jungol*), which are thicker and saltier, are set in the middle of the table for everyone to share.

There usually will be at least one type of *kimchi* (spicy dish) on the table. Often there are two or three, depending on the season. Like the rest of the food, kimchi is laid out in the middle of the table for everyone to share. *Mit banchan*—a variety of smaller side dishes, anything from pickled seafood to seasonal vegetables—rounds out the regular meal.

There are no real "courses," per se, in Korean meals. Generally, all the food is laid out on the table at the same time (or brought out when ready) and eaten in whatever order you wish. If you order *galbi* (short ribs) or other meat you cook yourself on a tabletop grill, they will bring your rice last, so that you don't fill yourself up too fast. When you have *hwae* (raw fish), they will bring you a starter, the fresh fish, and then a *mae-un-tahng* (spicy hot pot) made from whatever is left of your fish. Also, there is no such thing as dessert in a Korean tradition meal.

RICE

ENGLISH	PRONUNCIATION	KOREAN
rice	bap	밥
five-grain rice	ogok bap	오곡 밥
traditional meal with side dishes	hanjeongshik	한정식
mixed rice bowl	bibimbap	비빔밥
stone-pot mixed rice bowl	dolsot bibimbap	돌솥비빔밥
fried rice	bokkeum bap	볶음밥
kimchi fried rice	gimchi bokkeum bap	김치볶음밥
rice with black-bean sauce	jja jahng bap	짜장밥
rice with sweet-potato noodles	japchae bap	잡채밥
rice topped with sliced beef	boolgogi dup bap	불고기덮밥
mixed rice with raw fish	hwaedup bap	회덮밥
rice topped with spicy squid	ojingeuh dup bap	오징어덮밥
rice wrapped in seaweed	gimbap	김밥

NOODLES

ENGLISH	PRONUNCIATION	KOREAN
hand-cut knife noodles	kal guksu	칼국수
chicken knife noodles	dak kal guksu	닭칼국수
seafood knife noodles	haemul kal guksu	해물칼국수
"party" noodles (somen in broth)	janchi guksu	잔치국수
spicy mixed buckwheat noodles	bibim naengmyeon	비빔냉면
buckwheat noodles in a cold broth	mul naengmyeon	물냉면
cold noodles in soybean broth	kohng guksu	콩국수
spicy thick noodles	jjol myeon	냉면
noodles with black-bean sauce	jja jajng myeon	짜장면
spicy noodle soup with seafood	jjamppong	짬뽕
ramen	lamyeon	라면
dough flake soup	sujebi	수제비
potato dough flake soup	gamja sujebi	감자수제비
kimchi dough flake soup	gimchi sujebi	김치수제비
sweet potato noodles	japchae	잡채

MEAT

ENGLISH	PRONUNCIATION	KOREAN
marinated sliced beef	boolgogi	불고기
spicy sliced pork	dwaeji boolgogi	돼지불고기
beef short ribs	galbi	갈비
unseasoned short ribs	seng galbi	생갈비
stewed beef ribs	galbi jjim	갈비찜
spicy pork ribs	dwaeji galbi	돼지갈비
sliced pork belly	samgeupsal	삼겹살
marinated grilled chicken	dak galbi/gui	닭갈비/구이
seasoned fried chicken	yangnyeom dak	양념닭

SEAFOOD

ENGLISH	PRONUNCIATION	KOREAN
raw fish	hwae	회
squid	ojingeuh	오징어
octopus	nakji	낙지
baby octopus	jjookkoomi	쭈꾸미
crab	gwe	게
spicy raw crab	gaejang	게장
shrimp	se oo	새우
hairtail fish	galchi	갈치
mackerel pike	ggongchi	꽁치
another kind of mackerel	samchi	삼치

ENGLISH	PRONUNCIATION	KOREAN
tuna	chamchi	참치
eel	jang-uh	장어
mackerel	godeung-uh	고등어
anchovy	myulchi	멸치
abalone	jeonbok	전복
oyster	gool	굴
mussel	hong-hap	홍합
seaweed (usually in soup)	miyuk	미역
seaweed/laver sheets	gim	김

SOUPS & HOT POTS

ENGLISH	PRONUNCIATION	KOREAN
spicy hot beef soup	yookgyejang	육개장
rice cake soup	dduk guk	떡국
dumpling soup	mandu guk	만두국
fermented soybean paste hot pot	dwenjang jjigae	된장찌개
thick soybean paste hot pot	cheong-guk jang	청국장
kimchi hot pot	gimchi jjigae	김치찌개
soft tofu hot pot	soondubu jjigae	순두부찌개
spicy seafood hot pot	haemool tahng/ jeongol	해물탕/전골
spicy fish hot pot	meuntang	매운탕
"army" stew/"Spam" stew	budae jjigae	부대찌개

FLATCAKES

ENGLISH	PRONUNCIATION	KOREAN
potato flatcake	gamja buchingae/ gamjajeon	감자부침개/감자전
green-onion flatcake	pajeon	파전
seafood flatcake	hameul pajeon	해물파전
mungbean flatcake	nokdu buchingae/ bindaeddeok	녹두부침개/빈대떡
kimchi flatcake	gimchi buchingae	김치부침개

KIMCHI

ENGLISH	PRONUNCIATION	KOREAN
napa cabbage kimchi	baechu gimchi	배추김치
cube white radish kimchi	ggakdoogi	깍두기
"bachelor" kimchi	chonggak gimchi	총각김치
water kimchi	mool gimchi	물김치
ponytail radish kimchi	yeolmu gimchi	열무김치
cucumber kimchi	oi gimchi	오이김치
green-onion kimchi	pa gimchi	파김치
mustard green kimchi	got gimchi	갖김치
white kimchi	baek gimchi	백김치

OTHER FOODS

ENGLISH	PRONUNCIATION	KOREAN
dumplings	mandu	만두
Korean blood sausage	soondeh	순대
seasoned rice-cake snack	ddeokbokgi	떡볶이
fish cakes	odeng	오뎅
"goldfish" bread with red bean	boong-uh bbang	붕어빵
fried dough flatcakes with sugar	hoddeok	호떡
drinking snacks	anju	안주
side dishes	banchan	반찬
rice cakes	ddeok	떡
rice porridge	jook	죽
red-bean porridge	paht jook	팥죽
pumpkin porridge	hobak jook	호박죽
red-bean shaved ice dessert	paht bingsu	팥빙수

BEVERAGES

ENGLISH	PRONUNCIATION	KOREAN
water	mool	물
milk	ooyoo	우유
soda/soft drink	eumnyosu	음료수
beer	maekju	맥주
Korean sweet potato "vodka"	soju	소주
milky rice wine	makgeolli	막걸리
rice wine	cheongju	청주
ginseng wine	insamju	인삼주
grape wine	podoju	포도주
fermented sweet rice drink	shikheh	식혜
coffee	keopi	커피
green tea	nokcha	녹차
black tea	hongcha	홍차
barley tea	bolicha	보리차
ginger-cinnamon tea	sujeongwa	수정과
Job's Tears (grain) tea	yoolmoocha	율무차
citron tea	yoojacha	유자차
plum tea	meshilcha	매실차
ginger tea	saeng gahng cha	생강차

Index

See also Accommodations and Restaurant indexes, below.

Photo **Credits**

p viii: © Cho Seong Joon / Aurora Photos; p 3 top: © Cho Seong Joon / Aurora Photos; p 3 bottom: © Cho Seong Joon / Aurora Photos; p 4: © Cho Seong Joon / Aurora Photos; p 5: © Cho Seong Joon / Aurora Photos; p 7 top: © Cho Seong Joon / Aurora Photos; p 7 bottom: © Cho Seong Joon / Aurora Photos; p 8 top: © Cho Seong Joon / Aurora Photos; p 8 bottom: © Cho Seong Joon / Aurora Photos; p 9: © Cho Seong Joon / Aurora Photos; p 11: © Cho Seong Joon / Aurora Photos; p 12: © TongRo Image Stock / Alamy Images; p 13 top: © Cho Seong Joon / Aurora Photos; p 13 bottom: © Cho Seong Joon / Aurora Photos; p 15 top: © Cho Seong Joon / Aurora Photos; p 15 bottom: © Cho Seong Joon / Aurora Photos; p 16: © Cho Seong Joon / Aurora Photos; p 17: © Associated Sports Photography / Alamy; p 19 top: © Cho Seong Joon / Aurora Photos; p 19 bottom: © Cho Seong Joon / Aurora Photos; p 20 top: © Cho Seong Joon / Aurora Photos; p 20 bottom: © Cho Seong Joon / Aurora Photos; p 21: © Cho Seong Joon / Aurora Photos; p 23 middle: © Cho Seong Joon / Aurora Photos; p 23 bottom: © Cho Seong Joon / Aurora Photos; p 24: © Cho Seong Joon / Aurora Photos; p 25 top: © Cho Seong Joon / Aurora Photos; p 25 bottom: © Cho Seong Joon / Aurora Photos; p 27: © Cho Seong Joon / Aurora Photos; p 28: © Cho Seong Joon / Aurora Photos; p 29: © Cho Seong Joon / Aurora Photos; p 31 middle: © Cho Seong Joon / Aurora Photos; p 31 bottom: © Cho Seong Joon / Aurora Photos; p 32 top: © Cho Seong Joon / Aurora Photos; p 32 bottom: © Cho Seong Joon / Aurora Photos; p 33: © Cho Seong Joon / Aurora Photos; p 35: © Cho Seong Joon / Aurora Photos; p 36 top: © Cho Seong Joon / Aurora Photos; p 36 bottom: © Cho Seong Joon / Aurora Photos; p 37 top: © Cho Seong Joon / Aurora Photos; p 37 bottom: © Cho Seong Joon / Aurora Photos; p 39: © Cho Seong Joon / Aurora Photos; p 40 top: © Cho Seong Joon / Aurora Photos; p 40 bottom: © Cho Seong Joon / Aurora Photos; p 41: © Cho Seong Joon / Aurora Photos; p 43: © Cho Seong Joon / Aurora Photos; p 44: © Cho Seong Joon / Aurora Photos; p 45: © Cho Seong Joon / Aurora Photos; p 47: © Cho Seong Joon / Aurora Photos; p 48 top: © Cho Seong Joon / Aurora Photos; p 48 bottom: © Cho Seong Joon / Aurora Photos; p 49: © Cho Seong Joon / Aurora Photos; p 51: © Cho Seong Joon / Aurora Photos; p 52 top: © Cho Seong Joon / Aurora Photos; p 52 bottom: © Cho Seong Joon / Aurora Photos; p 53: © Cho Seong Joon / Aurora Photos; p 54: © Cho Seong Joon / Aurora Photos; p 60 top: © Cho Seong Joon / Aurora Photos; p 60 bottom: © Cho Seong Joon / Aurora Photos; p 62: © Cho Seong Joon / Aurora Photos; p 63: © Cho Seong Joon / Aurora Photos; p 64: © Cho Seong Joon / Aurora Photos; p 67: © Cho Seong Joon / Aurora Photos; p 68: © Cho Seong Joon / Aurora Photos; p 69 top: © Cho Seong Joon / Aurora Photos; p 69 bottom: © Cho Seong Joon / Aurora Photos; p 70: © Cho Seong Joon / Aurora Photos; p 71: © Cho Seong Joon / Aurora Photos; p 75: © Cho Seong Joon / Aurora Photos; p 76 top: © Cho Seong Joon / Aurora Photos; p 76 bottom: © Cho Seong Joon / Aurora Photos; p 77 top: © Cho Seong Joon / Aurora Photos; p 77 bottom: © Cho Seong Joon / Aurora Photos; p 78 top:

© Cho Seong Joon / Aurora Photos; p 78 bottom: © Cho Seong Joon / Aurora Photos; p 79: © Cho Seong Joon / Aurora Photos; p 81: © Cho Seong Joon / Aurora Photos; p 82 top: © Cho Seong Joon / Aurora Photos; p 82 bottom: © Cho Seong Joon / Aurora Photos; p 83: © Cho Seong Joon / Aurora Photos; p 84: © Cho Seong Joon / Aurora Photos; p 90: © Cho Seong Joon / Aurora Photos; p 91: © Cho Seong Joon / Aurora Photos; p 92 top: © Cho Seong Joon / Aurora Photos; p 92 bottom: © Cho Seong Joon / Aurora Photos; p 93 top: © Cho Seong Joon / Aurora Photos; p 93 bottom: © Cho Seong Joon / Aurora Photos; p 94 top: © Cho Seong Joon / Aurora Photos; p 94 bottom: © Cho Seong Joon / Aurora Photos; p 95 top: © Cho Seong Joon / Aurora Photos; p 95 bottom: © Cho Seong Joon / Aurora Photos; p 96: © Cho Seong Joon / Aurora Photos; p 97: © Cho Seong Joon / Aurora Photos; p 99: © Cho Seong Joon / Aurora Photos; p 100: © Cho Seong Joon / Aurora Photos; p 106: © Cho Seong Joon / Aurora Photos; p 107: © Cho Seong Joon / Aurora Photos; p 109 top: © Cho Seong Joon / Aurora Photos; p 109 bottom: © Cho Seong Joon / Aurora Photos; p 110: © Cho Seong Joon / Aurora Photos; p 111 top: © Cho Seong Joon / Aurora Photos; p 111 bottom: © Cho Seong Joon / Aurora Photos; p 112: © Cho Seong Joon / Aurora Photos; p 113: © Cho Seong Joon / Aurora Photos; p 114: © Cho Seong Joon / Aurora Photos; p 118: © Cho Seong Joon / Aurora Photos; p 119 top: © Cho Seong Joon / Aurora Photos; p 119 bottom: © Cho Seong Joon / Aurora Photos; p 120: © Cho Seong Joon / Aurora Photos; p 121: © Cho Seong Joon / Aurora Photos; p 122 top: © Cho Seong Joon / Aurora Photos; p 122 bottom: © Cho Seong Joon / Aurora Photos; p 124: © Cho Seong Joon / Aurora Photos; p 125: Courtesy The Plaza; p 126: Courtesy Sheraton Grande Walkerhill; p 131: Courtesy Grand Ambassador Seoul; p 132: © Cho Seong Joon / Aurora Photos; p 133: © Cho Seong Joon / Aurora Photos; p 134: © Cho Seong Joon / Aurora Photos; p 135: © Cho Seong Joon / Aurora Photos; p 136 top: © Cho Seong Joon / Aurora Photos; p 136 bottom: © Cho Seong Joon / Aurora Photos; p 137: © Cho Seong Joon / Aurora Photos; p 139: © JTB Photo Communications, Inc. / Alamy Images; p 140 middle: © Anthony Plummer / Lonely Planet Images; p 140 top: © FilterEast / Alamy Images; p 143: © JTB Photo / SuperStock, Inc.; p 145: © JTB Photo / SuperStock, Inc.; p 147: © Cho Seong Joon / Aurora Photos; p 148: © Cho Seong Joon / Aurora Photos; p 149: © Cho Seong Joon / Aurora Photos; p 151: © Cho Seong Joon / Aurora Photos; p 152 top: © Cho Seong Joon / Aurora Photos; p 152 bottom: © Cho Seong Joon / Aurora Photos; p 153: © Cho Seong Joon / Aurora Photos; p 154: © Cho Seong Joon / Aurora Photos; p 155: © Cho Seong Joon / Aurora Photos